GATEWAY
CITY

Alex Mair

FIFTH
HOUSE
PUBLISHERS

Front cover painting "View of Edmonton from the North Saskatchewan River" by Alfred Crocker Leighton, courtesy The Leighton Centre and Glenbow Collection, Calgary, Alberta, Canada.
Cover and interior design by John Luckhurst/GDL
All photographs courtesy The Edmonton City of Edmonton Archives

The publisher gratefully acknowledges the support of The Canada Council for the Arts and the Department of Canadian Heritage.

THE CANADA COUNCIL | LE CONSEIL DES ARTS
FOR THE ARTS | DU CANADA
SINCE 1957 | DEPUIS 1957

We acknowledge the financial support of the Government of Canada through the Book Publishing Industry Development Program for our publishing activities.

Printed in Canada.
01 02 03 / 5 4 3 2

Canadian Cataloguing in Publication Data

Mair, Alex.
  Gateway city

  ISBN 1-894004-60-4

  1. Edmonton (Alta.)—History. 2. Edmonton (Alta.)—Biography.
I. Title.
FC3696.4.M34 2000   971.23'34   C00-910945-5
F1079.5.E3M36 2000

Fifth House Ltd.
A Fitzhenry & Whiteside Company
1511-1800 4 ST. SW
Calgary, Alberta, Canada
T2S 2S5

Contents

Historic
St. Joachim's Church

Wed hen considering historic buildings in Edmonton, there is nothing
that can quite match the significance of St. Joachim's Catholic
Church and the role it has played in the city's history.

It's easy enough to say, as Alberta Culture did in August of 1978 when
St. Joachim's was declared a provincial historic resource, that it is "The
oldest-standing Roman Catholic Church in Edmonton, representing one of
Alberta's oldest parishes." And it is also easy to point out, as the Edmonton
Historical Board did when it unveiled the plaque honouring St. Joachim's
in 1980, that "The beginnings of this church go back to 1854 when Father
A. Lacombe, OMI, built a house-chapel inside Fort Edmonton."

Of course both Alberta Culture and the Historical Board said more
than the simple statements we've mentioned, but still, the whole story is so
rich in local history that it is very difficult to wrap it up in a few sentences.

The first visit to Fort Edmonton by Catholic clergy was in 1838. Fathers
Norbert Blanchet and Modeste Demers, two secular priests, spent some
time here at the request of the Hudson's Bay Company while on their way
to Oregon. They were to found missions to help stabilize the situation with
the Natives and to maintain peace.

In 1842 Father Jean-Baptiste Thibault, also a secular priest, travelled
from St. Boniface to Fort Edmonton by horseback.

In 1854 Father Lacombe, who had first arrived in the area two years earlier, was given a small building inside the palisades by the Hudson's Bay
Company's chief factor, John Rowand, that Father Lacombe converted into
a house-chapel. This was the first chapel in Fort Edmonton. The same year,
Bishop Tache, in the course of a visit to Fort Edmonton, gave the little
house-chapel the name of St. Joachim. That was almost a century and a half
ago, and consider what Edmonton was like at the time.

That was also the year that John Rowand died suddenly at Fort Pitt on
his way to Norway House. Two years earlier, in 1852, Father Thibault
returned to Norway House due to ill health and Father Lacombe took his
place. Just six years before Father Lacombe's arrival, in 1846, Paul Kane had

1

*St. Joachim's Church, pictured here in 1906, is the oldest-standing
Catholic church in Edmonton, and what a story it has to tell.*

visited Fort Edmonton and described it in some detail and said the total
population of men, women, and children at the fort was 130 souls.

In another six years, in 1860, a man called Tom Clover arrived to pan
for gold. He found some on what became known as Tom Clover's Bar, in
today's Clover Bar district. It was another twenty years before the first
North West Mounted Police arrived.

And in this little community, the Mission of St. Joachim's began.

On July 20, 1876, the governor of the Hudson's Bay Company wrote to
Bishop Vital Grandin in St. Albert and told him that the house-chapel
would have to be removed from the fort. The old church was dismantled
and the lumber hauled about two miles to thirteen acres of land donated by
Malcolm Groat. The second St. Joachim's came into being on this plot near
Jasper Avenue and 121 Street, and the first mass was celebrated in this
church on January 14, 1877.

Father Constantin Scollen was named first resident parish priest, but he suffered a severe attack of cholera within a short time and was moved to St. Albert; Father Henri Grandin, nephew of the bishop, moved in and is usually regarded as the first resident parish priest.

You'll notice the names of the participants in this story are names that are woven into the history of Edmonton.

In 1883 the Hudson's Bay Company put some of its land up for sale and Bishop Grandin bought a block of it. This property became the site of the third St. Joachim's Church, which was built on what is now the Grandin Towers parking lot. Work on that church began on July 5, 1886, and was finished on August 22, though it was little more than a temporary structure.

Then in 1898, the year of the Klondike gold rush, the basement of the fourth St. Joachim's was dug during the summer. The work was begun under the direction of Father H. Leduc, OMI, who was then the parish priest. On December 8, 1899, the new church was opened for religious services.

Considering the church as an important historic site in 1978, the evaluator said, "This church is of historical importance to the Province for its unusual parish tradition, continuous from 1854. St. Joachim's parish is the oldest Roman Catholic parish in Edmonton and among the first of any denomination established in Alberta. Although the present church was the fourth St. Joachim's to be built, it was the progenitor of all other Catholic churches in this city and is the oldest-standing Roman Catholic Church in Edmonton."

And on the question of St. Joachim's architectural importance, the evaluator noted that "Because of its early Quebec church style with side pinnacles and features such as leaded stained glass windows and decorative interior wood panelling, it appears that this church is somewhat unusual in Alberta. The age of this church, its type of construction materials, and its near original exterior and interior appearance add to its architectural importance."

St. Joachim's Roman Catholic Church, 9920 110 Street, is a historic building that is a rich part of our city's heritage.

But Who Was
St. Albert?

Just north of the Edmonton city limits you find yourself in St. Albert. Somehow, we know that St. Albert has been around for a long time, but few of us have asked the questions that might explain why it's there and how the original town got its name.

It doesn't take long to discover that St. Albert came into being back in 1861, and we all know that Father Albert Lacombe, OMI, was a major force behind its creation. But why build a mission, as Father Lacombe did, so close to blossoming Fort Edmonton, which was just down the road?

To understand the reason for the establishment of St. Albert you have to know a little about Father Lacombe. Albert Lacombe was born in Quebec, in the parish of St. Sulpice, in 1827. He was a scholarly young lad, and started his formal education for the priesthood when he was thirteen before moving to Montreal. There he was enrolled at Archbishop Bourget's Palace. While in Montreal he met Father Georges Belcourt and heard his stories of life on the western frontier, and Lacombe's life was changed forever. Upon ordination in 1849, Father Lacombe joined Father Belcourt at the Pembina Mission. In 1852, we find Father Lacombe at the Mission at Lac Ste. Anne, working with the Native and Métis people to whom he devoted his life and energy. It's interesting to note that on his trip west from St. Boniface with a Hudson's Bay Company fur brigade his travelling companion was John Rowand, the chief factor at Fort Edmonton. This was the beginning of a life-long friendship between the two men.

While the Mission at Lac Ste. Anne was doing a good job, Lacombe felt that there was a need for another mission closer to Fort Edmonton, but located away from the fort and the Hudson's Bay people who were working there. He worked with the Natives and Métis, and wanted his new mission to be for them. In order to achieve this, he felt that they had to live and work apart from the white settlers.

During his visit in January of 1861, Bishop Tache's tour took him through Edmonton and Lac Ste. Anne. In conversation with Father Lacombe, the bishop learned of his dream of a mission near Edmonton.

Father Lacombe took the bishop to the spot he had in mind, located on the banks of the Sturgeon River in the midst of the classically beautiful rolling landscape. He did such an effective selling job that Bishop Tache agreed completely with the plan, rammed his cane into the snow, and announced, "This shall be the site of your new mission, and I will name it after your patron, St. Albert."

And that's how it all began: a stick planted in the snow on the banks of the Sturgeon River in January 1861. Things have changed a little over the years, but St. Albert began as a dream of Father Lacombe's well over a century ago.

In the following spring Father Lacombe arrived with the first twenty Métis families to make the move from Lac Ste. Anne. They built a log chapel that's still there today, the oldest log structure in Alberta, and then they turned to building homes and planting crops. That fall they took off their first crop and had twenty homes ready for occupation.

The Métis built a bridge across the Sturgeon River, the first bridge in Alberta, the historians claim. Two years after the founding of St. Albert the first of the Grey Nuns arrived and set about building a school and a hospital.

While we're on the question of firsts, the first hospital in the area was the Grey Nuns hospital in St. Albert. If an Edmonton physician wanted to visit a hospitalized patient in the middle of winter he had to hitch up his horse and ride his democrat all the way out to St. Albert to make the call. In 1893, six Edmonton doctors petitioned the Grey Nuns, asking that they build and operate a hospital in Edmonton so the doctors wouldn't have to make the nine-mile trip. The Grey Nuns not only agreed, they purchased an entire city block and went to work building the hospital that we know as the General Hospital. It opened in 1895 at 111 Street and 100 Avenue.

Ten years before that, in 1885, we had a telephone link from St. Albert to Edmonton. On January 3, 1885, Alex Taylor phoned Father Leduc in St. Albert and wished him a happy new year. A man called Narcisse St. Jean got on the phone at the other end and replied, "The people of St. Albert congratulate the people of Edmonton on telephone communications being established between the two places and wish the clergy and people a happy new year."

Three and a half months later the same group of people in St. Albert were using the same telephone line to warn their friends in Edmonton that they believed that there were 1,500 Natives on their way to the fort to take it over. It was a false alarm, as it turned out, but the thought was there.

Father Leduc had taken over from Father Lacombe in the spring of 1865, and Bishop Vital Grandin arrived that fall. In 1870 a group of men went to work and constructed a church worthy of a bishop; it was eighty-four feet long, thirty-two feet wide and had transepts on either side.

St. Albert lived a life of relative peace and quiet until 1960. Then came the four-lane paved highway from Edmonton, and things haven't been the same ever since. St. Albert became a city in 1977, and in 1980 Edmonton offered to annex St. Albert. The answer was, thanks for your interest, but no thanks.

In St. Albert they'll tell you that they are Alberta's oldest community, and they certainly make an interesting case for it. And to think that all this started with a stick stuck into a snow bank in 1861! It's the amazing story of St. Albert.

A Special
Christmas Dinner

The year was 1873, and there was a Christmas dinner at the Hudson's Bay Company's chief factor's house. The dinner was quite unlike anything ever held at Fort Edmonton in the past. But then the wife of the chief factor, Fort Edmonton's first lady, was quite unlike anything seen at the fort to that point. And that dinner and that first lady were quite different from anything that has been seen in Edmonton ever since. We have to tell the story of the hostess who held that Christmas dinner to explain why they were both so unique.

The lady's name was Elizabeth Victoria McDougall Hardisty, but her friends and family called her Liza. She would have been twenty-four years old at the time of that Christmas dinner in 1873, making the level of sophistication she achieved even more remarkable.

She was the oldest daughter of the Reverend George McDougall, one of the earliest missionaries to serve in what we now know as Alberta. She had been born, as a matter of fact, while her father was still training for the ministry in Cobourg, Ontario. When her parents moved west, Liza stayed in the east to finish her education at Hamilton College, but at the age of sixteen she joined her parents at a settlement called Victoria, known today as Pakan, about eighty miles downriver from Edmonton.

But to get from Ontario to central Alberta in 1865 when you are a sixteen-year-old young lady wasn't easy. She made the trip with her brother, and by averaging fifty miles per day, it took not days, but months. That was in 1865, and a year later she married a gentleman called Richard Hardisty who was working for the Hudson's Bay Company.

Richard Hardisty, her future husband, was a career man with the Bay. He was based in Rocky Mountain House at this point, but his travels took him to Fort Edmonton and apparently as far downstream as Victoria Crossing and the McDougall's mission, which is where he met Elizabeth Victoria. They were married on September 20, 1886, and set up house at Rocky Mountain House where they stayed until the spring of 1867, when the moves began. The first transfer for the couple took them to Fort

Carlton. They were based there for the summer of 1867 before moving to Victoria Crossing for the winter of 1867–68. They spent the winter of 1868–69 in Fort Edmonton and then went on a year's furlough. After their time away they returned to Fort Edmonton, where Richard Hardisty was made chief factor in 1872. And that's when Edmonton's first lady began to come into her own.

Liza Hardisty must have been a breath of fresh air for the Fort Edmonton people. She fired the cannon that welcomed dignitaries to the fort. She hosted dinners, and welcomed the young gentlemen of the fort to all kinds of functions in the chief factor's home. That home was a problem in itself, for although it was within the confines of the fort, it was badly in need of repair. It was built for John Rowand, and was known as Rowand's Folly. Liza Hardisty was planning a replacement for the Rowand residence, but she didn't wait for that to happen before she started making her personal imprint on the local scene. A classic example of this was her first Christmas dinner as wife of the chief factor, a dinner to remember.

As soon as the ice was out of the river in the spring of 1873, the order went east for the Christmas goodies that she wanted for the following December. There were English plum puddings on the list, as well as candy, lump sugar, and other treats unheard of in an isolated trading post.

When all those treats arrived with the fall shipment of supplies, Liza had them packed in a storage room on a lower floor and then locked the storage door. She understood the curiosity of small children and acted accordingly.

Finally it was Christmas, 1873, at Fort Edmonton. But with it came the ultimate nightmare of every hostess in the world. The meat for the dinner hadn't arrived. Venison had been ordered from local hunters, but they hadn't appeared with it. Then, just after dawn Christmas morning, the people in Fort Edmonton heard a commotion coming up the river. Two dog teams, each carrying half a deer carcass, arrived with the meat for the Christmas dinner that was to be held at mid-day.

At noon, December 25, 1873, the entire company of Fort Edmonton sat down to dinner in Mrs. Hardisty's home. They didn't start their meal until after saying grace, and as was customary at the time, the grace was a long one.

The "Old Timer" writing in the *Edmonton Journal* described the meal this way:

Metis girls served the meal: venison, wheat bread, potatoes, vegetables grown locally, dried Saskatoons that served as currants, lump sugar for the tea, and last but not least, plum pudding for everyone, and plum pudding from the old country, at that.

The same column tells us that after dinner more visitors began pouring into the fort. They were the Crees, coming to pay their respects to "Red Head" and his lady.

This was far removed from the usual routine of the fort. Normally it took days before the Natives could get into the stockade to trade their furs, but here, in the middle of winter, the gates of the fort were wide open, and the Natives were welcomed into the Big House. They sat on the floor and were served tea and cakes, and they even left gifts when they had gone: a rabbit's foot, a deer's tooth, and a few animal skins.

And that's how they celebrated Christmas at Fort Edmonton in 1873, and it was a Christmas that made history.

Edmonton— What's in the Name?

There are some interesting place names in this province, and Edmonton just happens to be one of them, although we don't often think about it a great deal.

When they were building the rail line east from Lacombe, the route took the surveyors through the colony of Blumenthal, a Swiss settlement. The surveyors were royally entertained by one of the local farmers, and a notebook from one of the surveyors talks about the food, the music, the hospitality, and the beautiful daughters of the host. The host's name happened to be Carl Stettler, so guess where the name for Stettler came from?

How about Waskatenau? That name comes from Cree, and means, literally, "the cleft in the banks." The name was chosen because the early settlers built on the edge of the banks of the gully through which the creek ran down to the North Saskatchewan River. They called the stream Waskatenau Creek, and so the town that grew up beside it became Waskatenau.

And the name game goes on. But what about Edmonton? Where does that name come from, and when?

Digging around in the files at the City of Edmonton Archives you can quickly determine that Edmonton House was built on a site chosen by a gentleman called William Tomison. You can also clearly establish that the buildings were staked out on October 5, 1795, but that's when the throat-clearing starts. It would be natural to consider that Edmonton dates back over two hundred years, and that our urban history began on that autumn day in 1795. Except that Edmonton House wasn't built where Edmonton is now.

The first Edmonton House was built downstream, about twenty miles from where we sit today. The original site was about a mile and a half upstream from the point where the Sturgeon River flows into the North Saskatchewan. The Edmonton House trading post was shuffled around a lot over the years, moving the site from one location to another in an attempt to find the right spot at the right time. We only ended up where we are today in the winter of 1812–13.

But relatively short distances, such as the ones we're looking at in this instance, are points to fuss over rather than a cause of great emotional upset.

The naming of the place fits into a pattern. Tomison picked the name, and he is probably the one who named it after Edmonton, the community in Middlesex, England, and for a very good reason—that's where his boss came from. The practice then, as it had been over the years, was to choose a place name that honoured one of the senior members of the Hudson's Bay Company, or the place from which they came. Tomison's superior was a gentleman called Sir James Winter Lake, who was deputy governor of the Hudson's Bay Company at the time. Although there is no direct documentary evidence proving this theory, it seems a safe bet to accept the Edmonton-Middlesex-Sir James Winter Lake connection.

But the controversy doesn't stop here. Professor J. B. Tyrell, in writing about the journal of David Thompson, says that the name "Edmonton House" was likely chosen by George Sutherland, who was paying a compliment to his clerk, John Pruden. Pruden, it seems, came from Edmonton, the one near London in England. But as Bruce Ibsen, chief archivist at the City of Edmonton Archives has established, Sutherland wasn't anywhere close to Edmonton House when it was first built. Sutherland was in charge of Cumberland House at the time, a long, long distance away from here, and

*Things were a little basic in 1884 when Fort Edmonton
looked like something out of an old movie, but that's the way we were.*

Bruce also points out that Pruden was working at Carlton House that winter, which is also a long way downriver from here. The records of the Hudson's Bay Company establish that Pruden didn't reach Edmonton House until May 20, 1796, or early in the summer of the year *after* that first Edmonton House was established and named.

And having verified all that, you might, while you are at the City Archives, have a look at a copy of the *Edmonton Bulletin* that was published as a special Christmas issue in 1908. There, on the front page, is a story with another name possibility, although I don't know whether you're ready for this.

This story tells of Joseph McDonald, who was apparently a grand-nephew of Mad Mckay and a guide for John Palliser. This is a story that grabs your attention. McDonald, a Highlander, came up the North Saskatchewan in 1805 in the company of a fellow called Monroe, who was a son of the Colonel Monroe who fell while fighting under Wolfe at Quebec. The two of them were working for the North-West Company, and as McDonald tells it, when they arrived here the place wasn't called Edmonton at all. He says it was called either Fort des Prairies or Hughes Fort. Hughes, the story goes, was a "wintering partner" of the North-West Company, and was with Macdonald of Garth and a man called Shaw in establishing the North-West fort here. Our narrator goes on to tell us that the employees of the North-West Company were largely of French extraction, and had trouble with the name Fort a' Hughes, which became to the French ear Fort Auguste, which in turn was twisted into Fort Augustus.

So there you go. There was a Hudson's Bay post here when McDonald came up the river in 1805, and we better give him full marks for company loyalty when he refused to refer to the place as Fort Edmonton and chose to call it after *his* boss, Mr. Hughes of the North-West Company.

So what's in a name? An interesting story, if you follow the many threads back through time.

Edmonton's Oldest Hotel

Tucked into a comfortable spot on the north side of Jasper Avenue, just east of 97 Street, sits a building that has more claims to fame than most. It is Edmonton's first brick building, and also Edmonton's first brick hotel—the one hotel in Edmonton that has been in continuous operation longer than any other hotel in the city. It's now called the Hub Hotel, but that hasn't always been its name. It was, for many years, called the Jasper House Hotel. On June 30, the hotel has its birthday. It is now well over one hundred years old, and it has a marvellous story to tell.

It was back on June 30, 1882, that a gentleman named James Goodridge first opened the doors to his Jasper House Hotel in Edmonton. Donald Ross opened Edmonton's first hotel, and that's what he called it— the Edmonton Hotel. Donald arrived in our part of the world in 1872. He panned for gold and didn't make much of a strike, but he nonetheless put down roots, built a house, and over time converted it to a hotel. In 1882 he added an annex to the original log building and expanded his facilities. At the same time Donald was expanding down at the foot of McDougall Hill, James Goodridge was constructing his hostelry up on Jasper Avenue.

So what drew Goodridge to Edmonton, and why did he go into the hotel business? James Goodridge was born in 1852 in a place called Vaughan, Ontario, just north of Toronto. He arrived in the Edmonton area to join his brother, Henry, who had been here since 1876. These people were pioneers in this part of the world. In 1881 we find James was running a boarding house on Jasper Avenue a little to the east of where he ended up building his hotel, and we know that he started work on Jasper House in 1882 and opened it June 30 of that same year.

Records at the City of Edmonton Archives tell us that the original building was thirty feet wide and twenty-four feet deep. We learn, too, that a kitchen addition measuring sixteen feet by twenty feet was later added at the rear of the hotel. We know, also, that it was a wood-frame structure with a brick veneer across the front. Now we get into a terminology problem. The Jasper House is described in many of the records as the first brick building in Edmonton, and the first brick hotel. It was also held to be the first brick building west of Winnipeg at the time.

Whether brick veneer and brick construction are roughly the same thing is up for debate, but we do know that the business prospered, and in 1884 he built an addition on the west side of the original hotel and hired a local mason called William R. West to do the work. This part of the building is reported to be solid brick.

And another word game we might play involves the words "hotel" and "boarding house." Either way, Goodridge was host to some long-term residents in his hotel as well as a great many visiting dignitaries in the early years of Edmonton. His hotel was the stopping and starting point for the stagecoach run from Edmonton to Calgary. That must have been a trip to remember, too. Five days on the road, four overnight stops along the way, and no paved roads between the two points.

One of the many interesting elements of the Goodridge story is the serious approach he took to the food served in his hotel. Jasper House was the first institution in Edmonton to cater on a regular basis. In later years, even some of the rival hotels in town would turn to the Jasper House kitchen for the food they served on special occasions.

Away back in October of 1884, when Lieutenant-Governor Dewdney

The neighbourhood has changed a little over the years but the original Jasper House is still in business.

14

came to town, they held the reception and dinner at the Jasper House. The chef went all out, and served the guests a dinner built around three kinds of roast fowl, beef, ham, and assorted vegetables.

Good food and good service were very much a part of the Goodridge approach. But over the years things changed a little and the bar business became more important. You could sit down and relax with a glass of cold beer if the mood so struck you. We're back in the days when it was deemed inappropriate for men and women to polish off an ale in each other's company, so the Jasper House, like all other hotels, had a women's section and a men's section, accessible through separate entrances of course. In those early years the main east entrance led you into the ladies' bar. There were only five tables in the ladies' area, but there was a bit more room over on the men's side. To get into the men's area you used the entrance on the opposite side of the building, the west door.

When full, the ladies' area could seat sixty, but there was space for twice as many men in their section. The price of a glass of beer at that time was ten cents. The bar had another addition not that common in Edmonton: an automatic glass washer.

The original building has gone through many stages of renovations, the most extensive being those carried out in 1905 and 1940. Leonard Goodridge, son of the original owner, took over the operation of the hotel after his father's death in 1900.

The name was changed to the Empress Hotel in 1920, and then to the Hub Hotel in 1940. And the Hub Hotel is still there today, just across the street from the Shaw Conference Centre. Think of the Edmonton stories that have gone in and out of that front door.

Mr. Goodridge must be smiling.

The McPherson and Coleman Stagecoach

It was July 24, 1883, when two men climbed onto the drivers' seat of a stagecoach at 10:00 AM and shouted at the four-horse team in front of them. They pulled away from the Jasper House Hotel just east of 97 Street and Jasper and headed for Calgary to begin another phase in Edmonton's link with the rest of Canada.

The two men were Ad McPherson and Jim Coleman. They took turns handling the reins on the trip to Calgary, and if we have ever had a pair of trailblazers in this city, McPherson and Coleman certainly fit the image.

River traffic from Winnipeg had begun with the arrival of the *Northcote*, the Hudson's Bay Company sternwheeler, in 1875. You could always *walk* from Winnipeg at the side of an ox cart, if you had three months you wanted to invest in the trip, or, after 1883, if you could get south to Calgary you had the CPR to take you either east or west. And so the two men, McPherson and Coleman, decided to introduce the first regular stagecoach line from Edmonton to Calgary. They would leave from the Jasper House Hotel, the one we call the Hub Hotel today, take five days to get to Calgary, and then return, taking another five days for the return leg of the journey. They planned it as a regular fortnightly service, and that's what it turned out to be, although it was never easy.

The two men placed an advertisement in the Saturday, July 21, 1883, issue of the *Edmonton Bulletin*. The ad, in its entirety, read:

> Royal Mail, passenger, express and fast freight line, making fortnightly trips between Edmonton and the end of the track via Peace Hills, Battle River, Red Deer City, and Calgary. The first stage of the above line will leave Edmonton on Tuesday next at 10:00 o'clock a.m. For particulars as to passengers, express, and freight rates apply to McPherson & Coleman, proprietors. Office in the Bulletin Building, Edmonton.

After watching a lot of western movies over the years, we all have a preconceived idea of what a ride in a stagecoach would be all about. When it comes to the trip to Calgary, though, we have it all wrong.

First of all, the original coach wasn't so much a coach as a wagon. And it didn't have a real roof, either. There was an arrangement not unlike the top on a convertible automobile that could be pulled over the passengers and freight end of the wagon to give overhead protection from the weather, but not much more.

The trip cost you $25.00, one way. The price doubled if you wanted a return ticket. That just covered your transportation costs, although it included one hundred pounds of carry-on baggage and four nights at stopping places along the way. The "stopping places" weren't five star hotels. You had to be prepared to camp if the need arose, because the end of the day could come at different locations along the route depending on weather and travelling conditions. You couldn't really call them road conditions because there wasn't any road. The stage made its way around sloughs, across swollen creeks, and through mud holes. They did get you to the end of steel at Calgary on the fifth day, though, and that was what McPherson and Coleman had contracted to do.

Winter travel was something else again, and of course there were the problems of spring and fall. Sleigh runners on the wagon might be a very good idea when they left Edmonton, but who knew what the weather would

There was a distinct shortage of parking meters on Jasper Avenue in 1890, but the beginning of a great city can be seen, if you look closely.

be like south of Red Deer four days later? And how do you switch from runners to wheels in the middle of Alberta?

The stagecoach would leave the Jasper House Hotel, make its way down to Walter's ferry, across the river and up the Old Fort Hill to the level ground leading south, and from then on it was a case of picking the best route under the existing conditions.

And if the travellers thought their worries were over when they reached the track at Calgary, the reports coming back from Jim Coleman tell a different story. In a piece in the *Bulletin* on August 4, 1883, the newspaper tells about the experiences of the travellers.

The Royal Mail coach got back from the end of track at noon on Tuesday, having taken two weeks on the round trip. On the out trip it reached Calgary on Sunday without mishap, and reached the end of the track on Monday afternoon about two o'clock, distant from Calgary thirty or thirty-five miles. The works had reached a point at which it was necessary to lay down another siding. While the party were still waiting, a train load of material arrived, and inside of half an hour a siding was laid down, a telegraph office established and messages sent. The passengers got aboard a flat car at six o'clock and started for the next siding, ten miles distant. There they would get into the caboose of a construction train and proceed to Medicine Hat where they would take the regular train to Winnipeg.

And we think we're having a bad time when the luggage is slow getting onto the carousel at the airport. But that's what it was all about over a hundred years ago, if you went to Calgary on the McPherson and Coleman stagecoach.

Edmonton's First Telephone

W e wish you all a very happy new year." Granted, that doesn't sound like the most dramatic sentence ever uttered, but it was the first thing ever said over a telephone line in Edmonton, and it was spoken on January 3, 1885.

A gentleman called Alex Taylor had opened the telegraph office in Edmonton, working out of a space in John Walter's home, where the Kinsmen Field House is located today. Alex was an imaginative fellow and had arranged for news of the world to be sent to him by telegraph from Winnipeg. It was these written reports from the rest of the world that were posted on the wall of Frank Oliver's general store on the north side, which later led Frank to start the first newspaper in this part of the world, the *Edmonton Bulletin*, on December 6, 1880. But that's another story.

That greeting, made by Alex Taylor over his newly completed telephone line to St. Albert, was directed to the Reverend Father Leduc. Father Leduc didn't reply himself, but a man called Narcisse St. Jean did, and Narcisse said, "The people of St. Albert congratulate the people of Edmonton on telephone communication being established between the two places and wish the clergy and people a happy new year." And from that simple beginning, over one hundred years ago, came the system that we today refer to as Telus.

Taylor connected his office with the fort and a variety of business operations in town. Very quickly, Edmonton businessmen began to realize that telephones could give them an edge in their operations, and the demand for more and more connections came into Taylor's office. All of this, remember, came only eight years after Alexander Graham Bell made his first call from Brantford to Paris, Ontario.

The privately owned system was sold to the City of Edmonton in 1904, which in its own way, was the start of Edmonton Telephones, the municipal communications system.

There were a number of famous players involved with the system in its early years. The very first telephone operator was Janet Lauder. She was the daughter of Jimmy Lauder, who was the first baker in Edmonton. Janet, in later years, married a fellow called William Griesbach, and Billy Griesbach played a major role in the growth of things in the city during his lifetime.

The list of "firsts" for our local telephone system is impressive. It was away back in 1908 that automatic telephones were first introduced to Edmonton subscribers, and that put us right at the forefront of telecommunication technology in Canada.

Two years later the system introduced another innovation to the local scene. It erected emergency call boxes throughout the city, something that was unheard of at the time.

We were the first city in Canada to have touch-tone dialling, and you may be surprised to learn that we already had this new service in 1967. We were also the first city in Canada to put a commercial fibre optics system into operation.

We often hear comments about the number of telephone calls that Canadians make in comparison with the rest of the world, and it leaves us wondering how we have ever found the time to do much else in our busy lives. But again, look to Edmonton for a leadership role in the use of the telephone across Canada.

Back in 1936 Edmonton had twice as many telephones per capita as any other city in North America. That was due, in part, to the availability and the cost per telephone, but a large factor was the quality of the service. By 1980, the number crunchers tell us, Edmonton had one telephone for every 1.15 persons living in the city, and that, in itself, is an amazing statistic.

The Edmonton telephone system has also had an architectural presence in the city over the years. Its buildings in various parts of town were built to last, and you can see many of them in use today, although not necessarily as part of the phone system.

One of the illustrations in a 1914 collection of Edmonton photographs shows the North Side Exchange. It's one of those Edmonton buildings that always looks familiar, but you can't remember just where you've seen it. This one, if you're a north side driver, is one you have passed many times— it's on the southwest corner of 101 Street and 112 Avenue. Long after it stopped being part of the telephone system, the building served as the home for the City of Edmonton Archives, and after the archives moved to the Prince of Wales Armouries the old building was redone to become part of a rehabilitation program for the city hospital system.

All in all, Edmonton has been well served by its telephone system, ever since that day one hundred-odd years ago when Alex Taylor called St.

Albert and wished them all a happy new year. And he did it without the use of a cellular phone at that.

It is interesting to look back at the growth of the service we have today, with call forward, call display, call waiting, and all the rest. But it is also a rather frightening challenge to look ahead into the future of communication technology. If a hand-held cell phone can be linked to the Internet can we program the computer so that the phone doesn't ring just after we've settled down at the supper table?

The Night the Drums Stopped

It was Friday evening, March 27, 1885, and Frank Oliver went for a walk through the warm spring evening. He brought a newspaper, the *Edmonton Bulletin*, to Edmonton in 1880, and there was no shortage of things to write about for the benefit of his readers. The old issues of Oliver's newspaper give us an amazing picture of this city from over one hundred years ago.

Oliver's local news paints a clear picture of the Edmonton of 1885. We were a small village of 125 souls, clustered around the old fort that really wasn't a fort at all. His column of local news in the March 7, 1885, paper reports, "Spring weather. Slight rain last night. No school on Friday, owing to the illness of the teacher."

One of the interesting things about Frank Oliver was that you were never quite sure whether he was teasing you with his comments or whether they were to be taken seriously. On the front page of the March 14, 1885, issue we read, "One day last week a pet bear kept by F. D. Wilson of the Hudson's Bay Fort, came out of the den where he had been passing the winter to get a whiff of the spring breezes. Mr. Wilson, thinking he might be thirsty, gave him a drink of water, which the animal took readily and almost immediately lay down and died. A frightful example of the effects of drinking cold water."

We have a tendency to assume that exciting things have happened in other parts of the world, but not in staid old Edmonton. The night that Frank Oliver went for a walk was just the beginning of a period in Edmonton's history that people at the time believed would threaten every man, woman, and child in the area of Fort Edmonton. The events read like the story line of a great drama, and it all happened right here in dull old Edmonton.

News of the rest of the world came by telegraph from the east. Riders and travellers brought first-hand reports, all of which was fine, but there were ominous overtones to the stories about Louis Riel, Gabriel Dumont, and the growing tension in western Canada.

The *Edmonton Bulletin* carried all the news of the area, not just the threatening reports of the anger and frustration of the Native and Métis people who were trying to adjust to a changing world that seemed to be leaving them on the outside looking in.

Saturday, March 21, 1885: "Roads bad. Wintry this morning. Streets in town are getting dry. Water is running on the ice of the river at both sides. Joseph Macdonald saw six geese at the Pipestone Creek on Sunday last, and a number of ducks were seen at St. Albert on Wednesday."

But on the same page of this small newspaper were stories that had very threatening overtones. "Battleford, March 20, 1885: A police courier left Carlton at eight o'clock last evening, and arrived here this morning, bringing despatches saying that the rebels had seized Indian Department stores at the South Branch and made Indian Agent Lash a prisoner."

Later that day a telegram came through reporting that the Métis had attacked at Duck Lake the day before. "Ten police killed," the report stated. "Louis Riel and Gabriel Dumont victorious."

And then the line went dead. It had been cut somewhere between Fort Edmonton and points east.

And all that information, most of it threatening, must have been running through the mind of Frank Oliver on that March evening. J. G. MacGregor tells us, in his book *Edmonton: A History*, that years after the excitement had died down, Frank Oliver would reminisce about his walk

Inside Fort Edmonton the business of keeping the peace was rather basic, but the North West Mounted Police were ready for almost anything that might come their way.

that March evening. His office was very close to where the Macdonald Hotel sits today, and his stroll took him to the west end of the settlement. He was going to Norris and Carey's store, which was located at about 99 Avenue and 111 Street.

As he walked along the path that took him through one of the Native campsites on his way to the store, the rhythm of their drums filled the air. While he was at Norris and Carey's store, he struck up a conversation with a couple of the older residents of Edmonton, Bill Cusp and Jim Gibbons, who were already in the store when Oliver arrived. Their talk naturally touched on the frightening news of the battles to the east. They also considered the possibility of the troubles reaching Fort Edmonton. As long as the drums were pounding, storekeeper Carey said, there was no danger of an attack locally. It was a reflection of Anthony Eden's "Peace In Our Time" comment years later. Remembering his conversation that March evening, Oliver said he remembered Carey saying, "When the Indians go to war, the first thing they do is put their families in safety at a distance from the scene of action. If the Indians meant mischief now, the tents wouldn't be set up in town. As long as we can hear the drums, there can be no danger."

Comforted by that information, Frank Oliver made his way back to the *Bulletin* office, listening to the rhythm of the drums as he walked. In fact, as he drifted off to sleep that night, he could still hear the drums around Fort Edmonton.

And when Frank Oliver got up the next morning there was no sound of drums, there was no sign of the Native camps, and there was no sign of the Natives. They had vanished in the night.

The misunderstanding and confusion about what was taking place wasn't limited to the people in Fort Edmonton. The Indian population were trying to sort out the state of affairs and were reacting accordingly. Both groups were opposed to any violence, but the situation could, in today's terms, be defined as a massive breakdown in communication.

Saved by the
Field Force ... Sort of

It was Friday, May 1, 1885, when the Alberta Field Force marched down the Old Fort Hill on the south side of the river. They had come to save the good people in Fort Edmonton. It had been a frantic march up from Calgary and a tension-filled time for Fort Edmonton leading up to their trip. The interesting point of the whole exercise is that they might just as well have saved their energy. The crisis they came to deal with had never existed in the first place.

This was 1885, though, and the only telephone line ran from Edmonton to St. Albert. There was a telegraph, true, but when the wires were cut and the flow of news stopped, well, people being what they are, they just let their imagination run away with things.

The tension in the west had been building for a long time. The Natives were unhappy about the disappearing buffalo herds and the treatment they were getting from the Federal Government and its employees. The Métis were having a difficult time adjusting to an agricultural lifestyle, and things in general were terribly tense. Into this tangle came Louis Riel, called back from exile in the United States; when his return was coupled with the conversations held between the Cree Leader, Big Bear, and Crowfoot, the leader of the Blackfoot, people began to worry. News of all this trickled into Fort Edmonton by word-of-mouth from travellers, from the pages of Frank Oliver's *Edmonton Bulletin*, and from the telegraph line from the east.

On March 27 of that year, the telegraph had brought an ominous message: "Metis attacked at Duck Lake yesterday. Ten police killed. Louis Riel and Gabriel Dumont victorious."

And what was the scene like right here in Edmonton? If we turn to the pages of Jim MacGregor's book *Edmonton: A History* we find out: "Fort Edmonton was such a little settlement, and so isolated. Its white adults added up to 125. Within one day's march lived between five hundred and a thousand Indian men, all practised warriors, and probably ready to join hands with them were some five hundred Metis from St. Albert, Victoria and other nearby settlements."

And where were the North West Mounted Police while all this was taking place? They were all out at Fort Saskatchewan, because that's where their main base was, not at Fort Edmonton at all. The men in the Fort Edmonton area had a few rifles, and there were two brass cannon at the fort, but until this "rebellion" began to bubble, there hadn't been much concern about civil defence. As the tension mounted, Fort Edmonton organized the Edmonton Volunteer Company under the command of a local former soldier, William Stiff. He was placed in command of the EVC, which consisted of thirty men, twelve muzzle-loading rifles, and the two brass cannon at the fort.

At the end of March the news was all bad. Out at Fort Saskatchewan, the NWMP commander, Captain Griesbach, was swearing in special constables and arranging for the people living in the surrounding area to move into the police compound. He then made a trip to Edmonton to see how we were doing as far as defence plans were concerned.

As we moved into April, things grew increasingly tense. The *Bulletin* describes what happened next in this way:

> On Saturday evening, April 11, a report was circulated, carried from Fort Saskatchewan to St. Albert, and then telephoned to Edmonton, that 1,500 Indians had attacked Fort Saskatchewan at 3:00 o'clock. This caused a great stampede of families towards Edmonton and St. Albert, which kept up most of Saturday and Sunday. By evening the greatest part of the south side settlers had come over to the north side.

Attempts were made to reinforce the palisade at the fort. Arms and ammunition were sorted. Food and water were stockpiled inside the fort, as Edmonton got ready to defend itself against the attackers.

But then, on Sunday afternoon, a report came in from the Victoria settlement, saying, "The news of the attack on Fort Saskatchewan was a humbug." Frank Oliver came out with a comment in his paper that is, today, a masterpiece of understatement. He noted: "This did a great deal to allay excitement."

Within a week, people were beginning to ask themselves what all the fuss had been about. But in the meantime, Edmonton had sent for help. On April 7, when the tension was really building, a group of Edmonton men decided to send to Calgary for support from the army. The only way to get a request for help to Calgary was in the form of a dispatch taken by a good man on a fast horse. The good man was James Mowatt, and the first fast horse was replaced by other horses as Mowatt made his way south. He started his long ride on the night of April 8 with a message to General Strange in Calgary.

Mowatt knew that his route would take him through territory held by six separate tribes, and each of them, presumably, was in favour of the rebellion and would not look kindly on a dispatch rider going for help as he rode through their reserves.

Mowatt planned his trip so that it would take him through the various reserves in the darkness of a prairie night. And by riding hard for thirty-six hours he reached Calgary and handed the dispatch to General Strange. That was at noon on April 10. A telegram from Calgary was sent to General Middleton who responded quickly, ordering troops to be sent to Edmonton. Strange sent what he could, a unit of twenty men under the command of General Sam Steele.

In the meantime, James Mowatt acquired another horse, saddled up and headed right back to Edmonton, bearing the news that help was on the way. But it wasn't until May 1 that the first echelon of troops came marching down the Old Fort Hill towards Walter's ferry, determined to end the crisis that had never existed in the first place.

All of which proves the importance of good communication systems in this world of ours.

The Man
Who Was Mayor

The media have spent considerable time and space over recent years discussing the image of the elected members of our city council. It's interesting to reflect on the fact that it was in 1892 that Edmontonians were first thinking about a mayor and town councillors. And what kind of man did they pick for the mayor's chair back then? Well they picked a character, a real character. And they didn't have to vote him into office. Nobody ran against him, and he was elected by acclamation. He was, without a doubt, the people's choice.

His name was Matt McCauley, but who was he, where did he come from, and why was he the unanimous choice of the Edmonton electorate?

McCauley arrived in our part of the world in October of 1879, walking beside a wagon from Winnipeg. He tried farming in the Fort Saskatchewan area for a few years, but moved to Edmonton in 1881 and opened a stable.

There are a couple of stories that tell us a great deal about Matt McCauley. Actually, there are countless stories about McCauley, but two in particular give us some insight into the man.

In March 1882, the year after he moved to Edmonton, the local people were looking forward to the arrival of the Dominion land survey. After the local area had been surveyed, they could claim title to the land that, in many cases, they had been living on for years. One of the local residents, Richard Hardisty, the chief factor for the Hudson's Bay Company, had his eye on a choice parcel about where the convention centre sits today. This didn't make any difference to a fellow called J. L. George, who built himself a shack on what Hardisty felt was his property, and George refused to move. Some of the other townsfolk felt that Hardisty was right, so they, too, spoke to Mr. George, who still refused to move.

Then a delegation took the matter to Matt McCauley, and Matt spoke to Mr. George who, again, declined to move. So Matt McCauley gathered a small group of husky supporters and they simply pushed Mr. George's shack over the edge of the riverbank and watched it fly to pieces as it thumped down towards the water.

*In 1884 Matt McCauley (centre) and his friend Chief Ermine Skin posed
with a North West Mounted Policeman in downtown Edmonton.*

This, then, was the "image" of the man that Edmontonians decided
should be our first mayor. He took office in early 1892. It was in June of that
same year that the Matt McCauley we're beginning to understand went
into action again.

There was a tremendous amount of rivalry between the two communities that existed here in 1882: Strathcona on the south side and Edmonton
on the north. Strathcona had the terminus of the railroad that ran up from
Calgary. But people there felt that, to enhance the value of their real estate,
they should have a government office in Strathcona as well. The Land
Titles Office was in Edmonton, and Strathcona wanted it, so the community petitioned Ottawa to get it. Wasn't it a shame that all these new settlers, in order to check their land claims, had to get off the train in
Strathcona, make their way down the hill, across the river on the ferry, and
all the way up the hill on the other side? Ottawa agreed, and directed
"Timber" Tom Anderson, the local Land Titles officer, to move his operation to the south side.

Anderson knew this was a political football, so he waited until
Saturday afternoon, June 18, 1882, to make his move. But a road mainte-
nance crew spotted the wagon outside the Land Titles Office with

Anderson loading the records. They notified Matt McCauley.

Mayor McCauley knew precisely what was going on. So he rounded up his "vigilantes" again, who marched down and formed an armed ring around the Land Titles Office, pointing out the lack of wisdom in Anderson's endeavours. To reinforce their point of view, they unhitched the team of horses and led them away, and then to underline their point, they took the wheels off the wagon.

Telegrams flew between Edmonton and Ottawa. Ottawa sent an order to Major Griesbach, in charge of the NWMP detachment in Fort Saskatchewan, to ride to Edmonton with an armed force and put down this insurrection.

McCauley met Griesbach's troop about where Commonwealth Stadium exists today, and again McCauley made his point, noting to Major Griesbach that if the armed troop proceeded into Edmonton, there would be bloodshed. Griesbach agreed and held up his men at the Rat Creek site, and more telegrams flew to Ottawa.

On Monday, Ottawa blinked. The Land Titles Office stayed where it was, there wasn't a shot fired, and Edmonton's mayor had carried the day.

The Water-carrier

He was born at Lac Ste. Anne in 1853, and he died in St. Albert eighty-six years later. In between he created one of the more colourful chapters in Edmonton's history. He had many names, officially and unofficially, but was best known as Muchias, the water-carrier. He was barely four feet tall, but the legend comes from what he did, not how high he stood above the ground.

His father's name was Richard Collin; his mother's name was Genevieve Bruyeres. He was christened Mathias Collin by Father Joseph Bourassa at Lac Ste. Anne, although he was later listed as John Collins in the records of the Hudson's Bay Company at Fort Edmonton. He was also known as Little Henry to his fellow-workers at the John Walter lumber mill and boat yard, and one story has it that the name "Mathias" became "Muchias" through inept translation. It doesn't really matter what you call him—he is a fascinating part of the fabric that made up this city.

He went to work at Fort Edmonton at some point prior to the second Riel Rebellion in 1885. He actually carried water from the river to the palisaded fort using a wooden yoke that he slung across his shoulders. With the passage of time he moved up to a horse and stone-boat to carry barrels of water up the hill, and there are all kinds of stories of the tricks the boys of the fort used to play on Muchias. The favourite was to roll a large rock into the middle of the road that he used to haul his barrels of water up to the fort.

Muchias lived close to the edge of the North Saskatchewan River all his life and was as comfortable in the river as he was beside it. We know that on at least one occasion he dived into the water when it was at flood and swam out to rescue a child who had fallen into the stream. He was known amongst the local small fry, the ones who dearly loved to play at the river's edge, as the man who chased them away from the water with a stick.

He built himself a house on the south side of the river, almost in the shadow of the High Level Bridge, and fitted it with furniture appropriate to his size. The table, the chairs, the doorways, were all at a scale that fit Muchias.

Muchias became very fond of John Walter and his family, so when John

They called Muchias the water-carrier, but he became a legend in his own time and stood eight feet tall in the eyes of his friends and admirers.

died in 1920 Muchias adopted the family in his own way and kept an eye on Mrs. Walter and the two boys. Muchias's home wasn't too far from the Walter house, and with the Walter family and his river close at hand, Muchias felt that he was living close to his best friends.

There are all kinds of fascinating bits and pieces of the Muchias legend, but a story that hasn't been told at any length pops up in the pages of the autobiography of Major-General W. A. Griesbach. Billy Griesbach was the son of Major A. H. Griesbach, regimental number one in the North West Mounted Police, and Billy grew up in and around the Edmonton and Fort Saskatchewan police outfits where his father was posted.

Part of the defence of Fort Edmonton was built around two small, brass cannons. Griesbach, in his autobiography, tells us that the cannons, four pounders, were not mounted at first, but his father had them slung between two wagon wheels. Griesbach Senior discovered that the tins of salmon kept in stores at Fort Edmonton were exactly the same size as the barrels of the cannons. He gathered all the scrap metal from the local blacksmiths, filled the cans with the metal pieces, and then had the lids soldered back in place. When they tried these "cannon balls," they found that the range was about two hundred yards, and the effect of the do-it-yourself shrapnel was more than might have been wished.

As tension from the 1885 Riel uprising began to have an effect on the Edmonton area, Griesbach arranged to have the cannons used for target practice when there were Natives in the audience, and everyone seemed duly impressed.

The military answer to the uprising was to dispatch a column of troops from Calgary to assist in the defence of Fort Edmonton. The troops, under the command of General Strange, consisted of men from the 65th Carabineers of Montreal and elements of the Winnipeg Light Infantry. On May 1, 1885, Strange led his troops down the Old Fort Hill on the south side to the ferry at the edge of the river. The 65th, in their bottle-green uniforms, the scarlet of the Light Infantry, and the spring foliage made it a colourful sight at the ferry landing.

To honour the occasion, the two brass cannons were to be fired from the high ground outside the fort as a salute to the arriving troops. Muchias was one of the gunners.

The powder charge in a paper parcel was dropped down the muzzle and then rammed into place. They were not using the salmon cans for projectiles; they just wanted the big bang and the smoke. A small fire was built between the two cannons, and when they were to be fired a hot metal poker was drawn from the fire, pushed into the touchhole, and the powder exploded. Muchias, in the excitement of the moment, tried to ram a fresh charge down the muzzle of a cannon that was already loaded. The other gunner was busy touching off the powder when Muchias realized what was happening, and he jumped to one side as the cannon fired.

The double charge sent Muchias's ramrod sailing across the river and dropped it into the middle of the arriving troops, making a suitable welcome to Fort Edmonton.

Mathias Collin died on Tuesday, September 19, 1939, four feet high but eight feet tall.

Here's the News

We have a rather remarkable newspaper tradition in Edmonton, a point we often overlook. Frank Oliver published the first issue of his *Edmonton Bulletin* on December 6, 1880, making it the first newspaper in what was to become the province of Alberta twenty-five years later. The *Edmonton Journal* appeared on the scene on November 11, 1903.

What we tend to miss are the interesting stories of the other newspapers that have appeared over the years, and that have been a source of news and entertainment for generations of Edmontonians.

Radio came to town in 1922 when Dick Rice sat down before a microphone in a corner of the newsroom at the *Edmonton Journal* and brought his listeners the stories of those things that altered and illuminated our lives, as Walter Cronkite used to say. And it was the same Dick Rice, more formally Dr. G. R. A. Rice, who brought his Sunwapta Broadcasting Organization into the world of television in 1954.

Between 1880 and the introduction of radio, newspapers were the way we got the news. Along with the *Bulletin*, which served readers on the north side of the river, the people on the south side had the *Strathcona Plain Dealer*, and you may be surprised to find that it made its appearances on the newsstands in 1894. It first saw the light of day as the *South Edmonton News*, and subsequently changed its name to the *Plain Dealer*.

Frank Oliver was one of Edmonton's more colourful newspapermen, but we can't overlook Clarence Stout. He came to our part of the world and made a remarkable name for himself, beginning with the *Plain Dealer*. There is a nice photograph of the aldermen who met for the last time as the council of the City of Strathcona on September 26, 1911. The good people of Strathcona had voted to join Edmonton, and Clarence was there to cover the last meeting, looking very serious in the picture. He would have been one of those invited by Strathcona's mayor, Arthur Davies, to a wake that was held in the Strathcona Hotel. His privately published memoirs, *Backtrack*, are one of the great adventure stories of this part of the world.

We had *The Edmonton Daily Capital* for a while, and you could buy copies of all the papers, as well as out-of-town papers, from a sidewalk stand right on Jasper Avenue. It was owned and operated by a fellow called John Michaels, who started selling newspapers on the streets of New York as a

A newspaper's job is to bring the news to its readers, and the Edmonton Journal *did it the hard way during World War I when it hired a painter to recreate the front page of the newspaper on the side of a building.*

boy of ten. His operation became Mike's Newsstand, and old Edmontonians still remember his neon sign with the man sitting behind a newspaper and shaking his leg back and forth.

Not just the papers but also the people and the buildings in which they worked became part of our heritage. Frank Oliver came to town to make a living as a merchant. He had been in the newspaper business, but felt it was time for a change. He put up a log building on Jasper Avenue and whitewashed it, living upstairs and running his business on the ground floor. Across the river Alex Taylor was running the telegraph office out of John Walter's house, and brought clippings of the world news across the river and tacked them up on the wall of Oliver's store. Frank was canny enough to realize that people were coming in to catch up on the news and buying something while they were there. But the ink was still a little thicker in his veins than he realized, so along with Alex Taylor, Frank Oliver got back into the newspaper game. That whitewashed log building was a fixture on Jasper Avenue until 1894. Look for it today down on 1885 Street at Fort Edmonton Park.

There is an interesting photograph of the *Edmonton Journal* offices in a 1914 pictorial publication. The *Journal* offices are located on the ground floor of a building that is remembered as the Tegler Building. Robert Tegler built this landmark in two stages. The first stage was so successful that he carried right on with the second part of it, for which he needed the corner on 101 Street that housed the *Journal* offices. The newspaper had a lease, and their new building on 101 Street and 100 Avenue wasn't quite ready, so they said, rather quietly, that since they had a lease they weren't going to move until their lease expired, at which time the new building would be ready. Tegler appeared to be stymied. But he decided that the lease didn't say anything about the space *above* the *Journal* offices, so he went ahead and built the rest of his office building over and above the newspaper. When the paper moved out, he finished the building down to the ground on the space they had occupied.

Frank Oliver's *Bulletin* ceased publication on January 20, 1951. The other papers in town had long since stopped publishing, and Edmonton was a one-newspaper town (the *Journal*) until the *Edmonton Sun* appeared on the streets on April 2, 1978. And guess who came to Edmonton to be publisher of this new upstart paper? A gentleman called Ron Collister, a name still known, and respected, in the journalistic world of this city.

As a city, we have been well served by our newspapers over the years, and it doesn't hurt to stop and remember, from time to time, what an important part of our heritage they have been.

Never Fired
in Anger

Many of the photographs of Fort Edmonton have two prominent objects somewhere in the picture. The two items are cannons, and were obviously a source of great pride by the look of them. And while there have been all kinds of things written about the fort, the people in it, and the events that took place there, nobody has said very much about these cannons.

They are mentioned from time to time in some of the early stories. We know that Liza Hardisty, the wife of the Hudson's Bay Company's chief factor, was something of a character. And we know that when the cannons were fired as part of the welcoming ceremony when dignitaries came to Fort Edmonton, Liza loved to be out there pressing a burning brand into the touchhole on the cannon, and causing the dramatic explosion and burst of smoke.

But there doesn't seem to be much information about the cannons themselves—why they were at Fort Edmonton or what they were used for. Then, in the pages of W. A. Griesbach's autobiography, a book he called *I Remember*, the story begins to come together. And as is often the case, the more you read, the more fascinating it gets.

These weren't just ordinary cannons. They were *brass* cannons, four-pounders, and when W. A. (Billy) Griesbach's father arrived to take command of the North West Mounted Police detachment here, he found the cannons stored in the Hudson's Bay warehouse. They weren't mounted on anything; they were just lying there. So he had them set up on wagon wheels and arranged so that they could be fired. He discovered, as well, that while there was a good stock of black powder at the fort, nobody had thought about ammunition for these weapons. But a short while later, again under Griesbach's command and guidance, somebody discovered that the tins of salmon that were supplied to the fort for food stuff for the employees were round tins, and their diameter was just the same size as the bore of the cannon. Griesbach, his son tells us, ordered that whenever salmon was used in the kitchen, the empty cans were to be saved. He then rounded up all the old bits and pieces of metal from the blacksmith shop, had his men load the salmon cans with the leftover shrapnel from the blacksmith's operations, and soldered the lids back on.

All of this was prior to the second Riel Rebellion threat in 1885, and as stories and rumours about the impending uprising reached the fort, Griesbach would, in a marvellous example of psychological warfare, have his men practise firing the cannon. But this drill only took place when there was a large audience of Natives on hand that they might be duly impressed with the ferocity of these weapons.

It must have been very dramatic. Young Griesbach remembers seeing the guns fired in practise and how they would send a huge ball of white smoke out the muzzle, along with a loud bang, and the cannon would lurch back four feet or more as a result of the recoil. I think this would have had an emotional impact on anyone who saw it.

They needed *something* by way of defensive weapons if Fort Edmonton was to be protected. In his book, Billy Griesbach tells of General Strange discovering, while he was in Edmonton, that all the shot for the Snider rifles was defective. The rifles were sighted to one thousand yards, but the ammunition would only carry the bullets about two hundred yards. Strange dealt with the whole problem, Griesbach tells us, by ordering the men to wait until the enemy was within two hundred yards, fire their rifles, and then fix bayonets and charge. This, as Griesbach points out with magnificent understatement, was not exactly what the volunteers with the Home Guard had in mind when they had signed on.

Griesbach Senior must have been quite a character. Three or four times a year a judge of the Supreme Court would visit Edmonton and try all the civil and criminal cases brought before him. A problem arose because this was such a major event that all the members of the Edmonton bar celebrated so much that they were in no shape to appear in court. So Griesbach rounded up the whole bar association, which consisted of three lawyers, locked them up for three days prior to the court sessions, and then released them when they were needed.

In *I Remember*, Griesbach talks of the 1885 unrest and tells us that on May 1, 1885, General Strange led the Alberta Field Force down the Old Fort Hill on the south side to relieve what he believed was the siege of Fort Edmonton. Of course there was no siege, there was no uprising, but the force had come up from Calgary believing that there was. The force was made up of troops from the 65th Carabineers of Montreal and elements of the Winnipeg Light Infantry. To welcome the troops to Edmonton, it was decided that a salute would be fired from the cannons in front of the fort on the north side. One of the fort people involved in firing the salute was Muchias, the water-carrier, who got a little mixed up in all the excitement and left his ramrod poking down the muzzle of the next cannon to be fired.

Let the record show that the only projectile fired that day was Muchias's ramrod that sailed through the air and came down in the midst of the general's troops.

But it wasn't fired in anger, just confusion.

It wasn't quite a twenty-one gun salute, but Fort Edmonton had its own way of welcoming you in style, if the occasion demanded.

The Man
Made History

When you're reading about the early years in Edmonton, the name of Dr. Edward A. Braithwaite keeps cropping up. It isn't until you sit down and read about Doctor Braithwaite that you realize just what a unique individual he was and what a significant role he played in Edmonton's history.

Edward Ainslie Braithwaite was born in Yorkshire, England, on February 16, 1862. He came to Canada in 1884 and on May 7, 1884, joined the North West Mounted Police. When he left the police payroll on December 31, 1931, he had been on that payroll longer than any other man, living or dead. He served for forty-seven years and eight months. But how did he get from Yorkshire to Edmonton, and where does he fit into the Canadian story?

Edward Braithwaite was the son of an Anglican clergyman and was interested in pursuing a medical career. He attended the medical school at King's College Hospital in London, although he didn't obtain his medical degree until 1890 when it was granted by the University of Manitoba. That's a good place to pick up the story and to start filling in the interesting gaps.

For whatever reason, Dr. Braithwaite paused in his medical training and made his way to Canada. In 1884 he was in Winnipeg and enlisted in the North West Mounted Police as a uniformed member. We even know his regimental number—1025. He was sent to headquarters in Regina for further training where he did all the things expected of a recruit: the drill, fatigue duty, and even washing dishes in the mess. By virtue of the medical training he had received in England, he was designated acting Hospital Sergeant on September 1, 1884, an appointment that was confirmed on December 1 of that year.

In March of 1885, the Riel Rebellion had erupted and the decision was taken to send a column of men under the command of Colonel Irvine to the scene of the rebellion. Sergeant Braithwaite was designated to go with the column as medical officer. Although he questioned his own training

*Pioneers in Alberta's health care system had their own problems
to deal with, but Dr. E. A. Braithwaite was a medical man of
the times who showed us the way it could and should be done.*

and abilities, he decided to go, and the description of his experiences is best
given in his own words:

> On the journey up from Regina to Prince Albert I had twenty-two men
> snow blind and one frozen from the knees down. I placed his feet in a
> hose bucket full of water and covered him with horse-blankets in the
> sleigh. His legs were saved but he lost all his toes on both feet. The
> snow-blind men were treated with tea leaves.

Braithwaite and the column left Prince Albert for Fort Carlton with
about two hundred men in the contingent. Upon their arrival at Fort
Carlton they were told that the men who had been in the fight at Duck
Lake had arrived, and there were eight wounded men who needed
Braithwaite's help. For three days, Braithwaite was never out of his clothes.

The decision was made to evacuate Carlton, and in the process straw from one of the mattresses in the casualty room caught fire, and again the wounded men barely escaped with their lives.

They made it back to Prince Albert where the wounded received the care they needed and Braithwaite got caught up on the sleep that he so desperately needed.

He was sent to Batoche to look after the wounded there. He loaded the casualties onto the steamer that took them back to the base hospital, located about where Saskatoon is today. When he arrived at the police post, he saw Louis Riel being marched across the parade square, accompanied by Peter Houri, the interpreter, and a scout called Armstrong. Braithwaite didn't realize it at the time, but he was witnessing the arrest of the leader of the rebellion itself.

In eight pages of typed, legal-size paper, Braithwaite tells of his experiences in our early history, and you can't find more exciting adventure stories anywhere, or more authentic.

In a letter to the City of Edmonton in 1957, Assistant Commissioner George B. McLellan of the RCMP outlined Dr. Braithwaite's service. He joined, according to the letter, on May 7, 1884, and took his discharge with the rank of Staff-Sergeant on May 6, 1892. After his retirement, the letter tells us, Dr. Braithwaite set up private medical practice in Edmonton. He was appointed a contract surgeon to the force, in which capacity he served until November 16, 1911, when he was appointed an honorary surgeon by order-in-council. He retired from active duty as an honorary surgeon on December 31, 1931, but retained his honorary rank until his death.

Dr. Braithwaite became Edmonton's first coroner in October 1896, and served for nearly fifty-two years, longer than any other coroner in Canada. He was also Edmonton's first medical health officer.

He performed the first surgery at the General, the Royal Alexandra, and the Strathcona (University) Hospitals here in Edmonton.

Dr. Braithwaite has had a mountain named in his honour, and here in Edmonton, there is a park at University Avenue and 112 Street named for him as well. You don't capture the story of a lifetime on a bronze plaque on a stone cairn, but part of the inscription on that plaque reads: "Erected in memory of his outstanding professional service to the Indians, traders, early settlers and residents of Alberta." It hardly touches on the man's accomplishments, but at least it's a start.

Dr. Edward Ainslie Braithwaite—outstanding Edmontonian, outstanding human being.

Playing the Game

Today's skill-testing question is a tricky one: what is the oldest organized sporting activity in the city of Edmonton? If your answer was cricket, go to the head of the class.

Back in 1887, Edmonton businessman Richard Secord organized the first cricket league in the area, and the matches began down at Diamond Park. This was five years before Edmonton was incorporated as a town, and the total population of the area was estimated to be 350 people.

And in this, the City of Champions, the cricketers have held their own over the years. We don't often think of cricket in this part of the world, but that doesn't mean that it isn't an active sport.

Tucked into the cricket file at the City of Edmonton Archives there is a hand-written record of what we are told is "a match played at Edmonton this 19th day of April, 1889, No. 1 Eleven (E. Looby) versus No. 2 Eleven (D. Milson)."

When Edmonton was incorporated as a city in 1905, part of the celebrations included cricket playdowns leading to the Ochsner cup. (Mr. Ochsner was a successful brewer of the time.) The newspapers of the day ran a large picture of the Edmonton Cricket Club members who had won the cup, and a very distinguished group of gentlemen they appear to be.

Appearing every bit as serious but a little less distinguished is another picture of the players in a cricket match held just behind the Hudson's Bay store in the late 1880s. The names of the players are listed, and there are a lot of old familiar Edmonton names on the bottom of the photograph— Donald Ross, Alex Taylor, Dick Hardisty, and a J. Looby, whose name also appeared on that 1889 score sheet, along with E. Looby, so it's possible that the photograph of the players was taken at the same match that gave rise to the score sheet.

There is another sharp picture of a group made up of Edmonton City Council and businessmen taken down at the cricket pitch on August 17, 1927 (see below). Mayor Bury sits front and centre, and the list of players reads like the roster of the city's key players. Standing tall on the left side of the picture is Tom Garside, who served as city solicitor for many years. In the middle of the back row, looming large with his hat tilted at a rakish angle is A. G. Shute, the man who served as Edmonton's chief of police longer than any other individual before or since. To Shute's left stands A. W. Haddow, long-time city engineer, and to Haddow's left is Sid Gosling, the city claims agent, who in the course of his duties compiled a fascinating photographic record of the growth and development of a variety of city departments. As part of his role as claims agent, he was equipped with a huge view camera that took 8 x 10 photographs. Gosling not only made a photographic record of various accidents and claims, but he used his camera and darkroom equipment to capture events and happenings in and around the city. Some of Gosling's prints have taken on great historic significance with the passage of time. The two gentlemen in the 1927 picture who are wearing white lab coats are identified as the umpires.

The significance of this particular cricket match isn't noted on the photograph, an oversight that sends the curious to the newspaper files of the time. There was a great deal of sporting activity taking place in the city, most of which is reported in the papers of the day. The regular comics were Tillie the Toiler, Toots and Casper, and Barney Google. The Saturday comics were built around Maggie and Jiggs, The Katzenjammer Kids, and Mutt and Jeff. But no mention of a special cricket match.

Playing the game has been part of the Edmonton scene since the early years, and before hockey, or football, or baseball, we had cricket.

One of the other happenings in August 1927 was the visit of Edward, Prince of Wales, and his brother, Prince George. Edward seems to have charmed the city and everyone in it, and George, the shy one, gets a much smaller share of the printed page. Perhaps the city fathers and the local businessmen met in a cricket match to celebrate that royal visit.

One of the other remarkable entries in the Archives cricket file is the story carried by the *Edmonton Journal* in 1934. The *Journal* sent a reporter to interview an old Edmonton cricketer, Ambrose Dickins, and the reporter got more than he'd bargained for. "Hurry up, I'm going to play golf in fifteen minutes," was Mr. Dickins's greeting. Mr. Dickins was quite pleased to talk about his prowess on the cricket pitch, but wondered why the young reporter wasn't interested in Mr. Dickins's success in other fields—fields such as rugby, fencing, boxing, soccer, tennis, curling, hockey, pinochle, and yes, cricket. Mr. Dickins was seventy-four at the time, and went on to outline his trophies and triumphs to the startled reporter. A retired bank manager, Ambrose Dickins had one other claim to fame—his son was a bush pilot known affectionately as "Punch" Dickins.

And the cricket file ended on an ironic note. There is a Canadian Press report of the Canadian cricket team who went to England in 1954 that says, "Canada, which isn't considered good enough to play a top England team, has been travelling the lower-quality cricket circuit."

But then Pakistan upset England, and Canada began a three-day match against Pakistan at Lord's. "Where does England stand in the Commonwealth ranking if Canada should win?" huffed the *Evening News*.

To which Canada's player-manager Lew Gunn gave a typically understated Canadian reply: "This makes a very interesting situation. We have everything to win and nothing to lose."

John Walter— Orkney Entrepreneur

T. S. Eliot said it first, but he probably didn't realize he was talking about Edmonton at the time. Eliot said, "We shall never cease from exploration, and the end of all our exploring will be to arrive where we started, and to know the place for the first time."

The more you look around at the history of this city, the more you realize that it is one of the country's most colourful and interesting centres, and we often do indeed find that we are discovering it for the first time. Take John Walter, for example.

We know there are a Walterdale Hill, the Walterdale Bridge, and John Walter's old house, lovingly preserved, down by the Kinsmen Field House. We know that he came from the Orkney Islands in 1870 as a twenty-one-year-old with a contract to build York boats for the Hudson's Bay Company.

In the beginning, our rivers were our highways, and the York boat played a much more important role in our early years than we realize.

We also know that he introduced the cable ferry system to Edmonton in 1882 and that he built a riverboat that made runs upstream to Big Island. He called it *The City of Edmonton*, and when it was carrying a full load there were five hundred people on board, very likely enjoying the dance floor on the top deck.

But as you sit at a table at the City of Edmonton Archives reading about this man, and looking at the pictures they have on file, you slowly begin to realize that there is a great deal more to this individual than a cable strung across the river and a stern wheel river boat big enough for a dance floor on the top deck. This man was one of the early movers and shakers in Edmonton, and the more you read and the more you look at the pictures, the more you realize that you are beginning to know John Walter for the first time, and it's exciting.

Walter stayed with the Bay as a boat builder for five years, and then branched out on his own. He tried many business ventures, not all of them successful, but at least he tried. He worked with wood, so he opened his own lumber mill. He formed a partnership with William Humberstone in 1893 and the mill prospered, until in time John Walter bought out his part-ner and expanded on his own. In 1907 he opened a second lumber mill on the north side of the river, in the Ross Flats area.

He speculated in real estate, he opened a general store, he tried coal mining, and he gave back to his community through public service. He pushed for a public school on the south side, and served on Strathcona's first school board. He also found time to serve on Strathcona's first town council in 1899.

But it wasn't all easy. A flood in the North Saskatchewan in 1899 didn't quite reach his house, but it wiped out his mill on the south side. He fought back from that disaster, and by 1903 his mill employed over one hun-dred men and produced six million board feet of lumber. Nine years later, in 1912, that output had more than doubled. Then, in 1915, another flood wiped out both the Ross Flats mill and the one on the south side.

His coal mine business was a moderate success, but just after midnight, June 8, 1907, a fire broke out at the bottom of the main shaft. Before the night was over six men had died. The funeral was held outdoors at the cor-ner of Whyte Avenue and 104 Street. South side businesses closed for the event, and the funeral procession was over a mile long.

John Walter played a role in so many Edmonton firsts. When the tele-graph line was extended to Edmonton, the operator, Alex Taylor, set up his office in the Walters' home.

The sternwheeler *The City of Edmonton* served not only as an excursion boat but also ferried lumber from the Walter operations to points on the river upstream from Edmonton. He was an organizer, a businessman, a public-spirited citizen, and a strong family man.

And there must have been something about this man's character that touched the young woman from Ontario who came west to work at a summer job. It was a summer job that was going to pay her way to France to learn the skills of being a pastry chef, and so she signed on as housekeeper for Richard and Liza Hardisty, the Hudson's Bay Company's chief factor at the time. The young lady was Ann Newby, and she never did make it to France. She stayed here as the wife of John Walter.

Dull old Edmonton? Don't you believe it. The people who first came to this part of the world and stayed to make a contribution to it have left us a rich and exciting heritage. And we're getting to know it, and the place, for the first time. Eliot was right—even though he didn't know he was talking about Edmonton when he said it.

Crossing the River
the Hard Way

John Walter came to Edmonton from the Orkney Islands in 1870. He was twenty-one years old and had a contract with the Hudson's Bay Company to build York boats. He did just that, building York boats for the Bay for five years, and then he stayed in Edmonton and built a fortune and a reputation for imagination and accomplishment that still stands proud today.

That he lost his fortune through no fault of his own doesn't take away from the contributions that John Walter made to the community. He brought us many of Edmonton's "firsts," which include a coal stove and a reel of cable.

He installed the coal stove in his house in what is now called the Walterdale area, and it was Edmonton's first. His wife, Annie, had come to Edmonton to work as a nanny for the Hudson's Bay Company's chief factor Richard Hardisty and his family, intending to make enough money from her summer job to travel to France and learn the skills of a pastry chef. Instead, as we have seen, she married John and cooked on his coal stove instead. Another of the firsts attributed to John Walter was our cable ferry, which went on to become more than just a ferry during the years prior to the construction of our bridges.

John realized that getting across the river was a major problem that was crying out for a solution. He worked with wood, so he built a scow that was propelled by oars and used it to ferry people, animals, and goods across from the south side to the fort, which was located at that time about where the Legislature sits today. Some reports tell us that John powered the scow himself, and that is what must have led to the acquisition of the reel of cable and the use of the river's current to propel the ferry from one side to the other.

It's interesting to try and imagine what getting across the river was like before Walter's ferries were there. For a glimpse of what it was really like, we can turn to the words of another old Edmontonian, Matt McCauley.

The *Edmonton Bulletin* ran an interview with McCauley in its issue of November 1, 1913.

Before there were the ferries, the only way to get across was to get a big boat, haul it some distance upstream, then jump on board and row and pull as hard as possible so as to reach the other side, praying fervently at the same time that the spot where you would land would be within a reasonable distance of where you wanted to get.

No wonder John Walter decided that what the place needed was a ferry. In the same story in the *Bulletin*, John reminisces about getting the cable that he first strung across the river. And if you don't know how a cable ferry works, picture a flat-bottomed scow attached to an overhead cable with pulleys. When it's time to move across the river, the nose of the scow is pointed just a little upstream. The force of the current hitting the side of the scow pushes it ahead, and it's the current itself that moves the ferry across the river. When it's time for the return trip, the scow is pointed slightly upstream at its other end, and again the force of the current in the river pushes it across to the other shore.

But it was 1882, and you couldn't just stop by the hardware store and pick up a reel of cable. There wasn't one anywhere in the west, except in Winnipeg. So John Walter made a special trip to Winnipeg, picked up the cable, and brought it back on a Red River cart. He remembered installing the cable, and getting the cable ferry into operation in 1882. In that same *Bulletin* story in 1913, John talks about taking the ferry out of operation. "We took the scow out of the river last Thursday," he said, "and I hope we shall never have to use it again."

There is one part of the cross-river traffic story that we haven't considered. During the summer you could use the cable ferry to cross the river, and during the winter you could cross on the ice. But what did you do, particularly in an emergency, when the ice wasn't safe to use?

The answer is still there with the cable. They made a sort of basket that hung from the cable, and into it went mail, or a person, depending on what you wanted to get to the other side. Then the basket was pulled across by hand. It must have made for some interesting trips.

Beatrice A. Oakley, writing in her *A History of Early Edmonton* tells us that:

The Edmonton settlement was dependent on crossing in this more or less haphazard manner until shortly after 1876 when the pioneer settler, John Walter, established a ferry which plied across the river close to the Fort. It was a scow rigged with oars and when the river was high and swift the crossing was difficult. In the spring of 1882 the ferry facilities were improved by the stretching of a wire cable across the river, and the ferry was propelled over by this means. The scow was also lengthened to accommodate six loaded carts with animals all at once. The new wire rope ferry started on her trial trip in April 1882. The launching was witnessed by a vast concourse of Edmontonians. The boat was christened *The Belle of Edmonton.*

And that's the way it was, in the days before we had bridges to help us with our cross-river traffic.

Rush hour traffic wasn't a problem but getting across the river was, and John Walter solved it for Edmontonians with his LRT—Lightweight River Transit.

The Saga of
the Bush Mines

Marco Polo found it in China and refers to it in his travel diaries as "the black rock that burns." He was talking about coal, and for many decades coal played a vital role in the economy of Edmonton and the comfort and survival of the residents. It was the primary fuel for both heating and generating power, and we would not have survived without it.

Donald Ross gets the credit for being the first person to operate a coal mine in Edmonton. He was looking for something to keep the guests warm in his Edmonton Hotel, and he opened a coal mine, following a seam into the riverbank just below 101 Street.

By 1888 there were six mines in operation in the Edmonton/Strathcona area, and by 1907, between Edmonton, Strathcona, Clover Bar, and Namao, there were more than twenty in active production.

A file at the City of Edmonton Archives, dated 1910, tells us of the coal mine in the North Saskatchewan River Valley. It informs us that the common name for the operation was the Bush Mine, and that it was located on river lot 412. It says that the Bush Mine was organized by Edmonton Barrister P. Thomson, Kenneth Campbell, Harry Southgate, and Charles Laderoute. The file also tells us that there was a reorganization in 1922, and that the mine operated until the mid 1940s.

Mr. W. J. Dick prepared a report in 1914 dealing with the concentration of coal in Canada; he talked at some length of the mines in the Edmonton area. He tells us that another mine, the Humberstone, was situated on a mine spur of the Grand Trunk Pacific Railway, three miles from Clover Bar station. The Bush Mine, he says, was located on the North Saskatchewan River about a quarter of a mile from the Humberstone. He notes that the mine had no railway connection and that the coal was hauled by horse team to Edmonton for local use. The seam, he adds, laid flat and ranged in thickness from five to six feet.

The entrance to the seam was by a shaft that ran down thirty-eight feet below the ground surface. Some of the local mines were started on the side of the riverbank and followed the seam back into the bank. Some referred

Although Edmonton was sitting on top of enormous oil and gas deposits, until the 1930s the fuel of choice was coal, and the coal mine was an important part of the local scene.

to this method as gopher hole mining, but the Bush Mine was more traditional in approach. Mr. Dick, in his report, describes the operation this way:

> No power plant has been installed, and the hoisting in the shaft is done by means of a horse whim. The system of mining used is pillar-and-stall. The main entry is driven 10 feet wide, and the side entries 6 feet wide. The side entries are driven 150 feet apart and the rooms are driven off the side entries with 29-foot centres. The rooms are 15 feet wide and 75 feet long. No gas has been found in the mine and open lamps are used by the miners. Blasting is done by black powder and fuse. The mine has a capacity of about 40 tons a day but the actual average is about 10 tons a day. There are six men employed underground and three above ground. Ventilation is secured by natural draft and furnace.

And that was a word picture of the Bush Mine in 1914.

In 1921 a second Bush Mine was started near the end of Ada Boulevard and 36 Street. The miners here followed the coal seam in a generally northerly direction. A couple of Edmonton's more prominent realtors appear in the Bush Mine story about this point. McGrath and Holgate, the movers and shakers who brought the Highlands district into prominence in Edmonton, were mentioned in a story in the *Edmonton Journal* in which the activities of the two businessmen were discussed. The report states that "As well as their in-city projects, the partners bought up several hundred acres just outside the city limits, mainly to the north and northeast. A sideline was the Bush coal mine property, a 236 acre operation, that was bought for $200,000." This mine was operated in river lots 38 and 40 until 1943 or 1944, undermining a large part of Beverly.

An interesting social note tells us that during the Depression years the Town of Beverly started its own coal mine and used men drawing unemployment relief or welfare money to staff it. That report goes on to tell us that the population of the town at that time was made up largely of miners.

And on another social note, at one time we had a federal penitentiary in Edmonton about where Commonwealth Stadium sits today. The prisoners were required to work in a coal mine that began within the prison grounds, and the coal they mined helped warm the jail during the winter months.

In today's terms, when natural gas is the prime source of heat and energy, it's a little difficult to grasp just how important a role coal played in the life of Edmonton. But through it all, for many years, when it came to fuel, coal was king.

Keeping Your Cool in the Good Old Days

During a hot spell in late August, we all do the same thing at one time or another. We go to the refrigerator, get out the ice cube tray, and drop three or four lumps of ice into a glass. Then we add whatever fluid we choose to help ease the heat of the day, and sit back and enjoy it.

That's today. But there was a time in our history when it wasn't quite that simple. If you wanted to chill your drink you might have gone to the ice box and lifted the lid on the top. Inside, you would have found a huge lump of ice, melting happily away in the ice compartment, and with the aid of an ice pick you would have chipped off a few shards for your cold drink. An ice pick, in case that's a new term to you, was about the size of a small screwdriver and had a sharp point on the end rather than a flat surface designed to fit into the slot on a screw nail.

All of this is bad enough, at least in terms of home safety and sanitization in the kitchen, but it's where the ice came from that drains the blood from your face today. It came from the North Saskatchewan River, right in the heart of Edmonton. In this day and age you wouldn't put anything from the North Saskatchewan River in your mouth unless you boiled it for an hour first, and that doesn't do ice cubes all that much good.

This was a fairly common method of refrigeration, if you can call it that. The ice was there to be harvested, and there were companies that did just that: cut the blocks from the frozen surface of the river, stored them packed in sawdust, and delivered them to Edmonton homes all summer long. The blocks of ice went into wooden chests that had space for the ice at the top, a food compartment in the middle—very much like a small refrigerator today—and space for a pan underneath. Well after all, you had to catch the melting water in something. And if you forgot to empty the pan at night you would find yourself with a wet kitchen floor when you got up in the morning.

The system worked well. The ice wagon made regular deliveries on prescribed routes through the residential areas, and if you wanted the ice man to drop off a new block for your ice box, you simply put a little cardboard sign up in the front room window, letting him know that your ice supply was running low.

The harvesting process was simple enough. The crews sawed the river ice into long slabs, hooked a team of horses onto one end of the slab, and hauled it out of the water. The slabs were then hauled onto horse-drawn wagons that took the basic product to the storage house.

We have a record of ice harvesting in the river as far back as 1883. The price was certainly right in the early days. In 1883, a block of ice two feet square was cut from the river, hauled to your front door, and delivered to your ice box for ten cents. When you think what you can get for a dime these days, it makes that block of ice look like a real bargain.

There are photos on file at the City of Edmonton Archives that show the J. W. Huff crew hauling the big slabs out of the river in 1903, but the ice company most early Edmontonians recall is the Arctic Ice Company.

Their storage warehouse down in the Rossdale Flats area is still there, although it has gone through a number of users since it stopped storing ice. The company's red, horse-drawn wagons were a familiar sight on summer days all over town. On hot afternoons the neighbourhood telegraph would get the word out as soon as the wagon started down the street. When the

During a hot Edmonton summer, we had our own way of keeping our cool; it came from the North Saskatchewan River and made its way to our kitchen ice box.

ice man was making a delivery, small boys would climb into the back of the ice wagon and pick up chips to pop into their mouths to ease the heat and their thirst. That was melting river water you had in your mouth, and goodness knows what else besides the sawdust the ice had been stored in.

The ice man had a rubber cloak that hung over his shoulder and down his back. When he found out what size of block his customer wanted, he would chop it from a larger section, then, with the aid of a huge pair of tongs, he would swing the cut block over his shoulder and carry it into the house for the customer.

And thereby hangs the tale, in a sense, of the career of a young Edmonton man who ended his career with the Arctic Ice Company one dramatic summer afternoon. His name was Sid Raisin, and he was delivering ice to some customers on his route who lived in the Lambton Block on 97 Street and 110A Avenue. The caretaker at the Lambton Block tolerated Sid and his ice deliveries, but he didn't like Sid carrying the blocks of ice up the halls, dripping on the floor as he went. To keep the caretaker happy, Sid would carry the blocks up the metal fire escape at the back of the building and make his deliveries the non-drip way. But this was a hot day, and the block of ice was heavy. Sid got it to the third floor landing on the fire escape and put it down to give his back a rest. Then, when he was ready, he clamped his tongs onto the block, swung it over his shoulder, and turned to the door. But the tongs slipped and the block of ice went over the railing of the fire escape.

The block of ice fell to the ground, three floors below, and on its way down it took out every clothesline at the Lambton Block. And it happened to be a Monday, which meant that every line was full of freshly laundered clothes.

So that's how Sid Raisin finished his career with the Arctic Ice Company. And that's why we call them the good old days.

Ghosts of the
Columbia House Hotel

If you happen to be walking or driving in the vicinity of Jasper Avenue and 96 Street, pause for a minute and listen for the voices. There are more ghosts at that intersection than perhaps anywhere in town, and they're all laughing.

They're laughing because they have so many happy memories of the hotel that once stood on the north side of 101 Avenue, between the avenue and Jasper. It had many names over the years, but perhaps it is best known as the Columbia House.

One of the better-known guests at the old Columbia House was a gentleman called Jim Delaney. We have a very crisp photograph of Jim in front of the Columbia House in the summer of 1899. The story behind that photograph is just one of the legends that grew up around the hotel. Jim had taken the inland route to the Klondike when he was headed north to make his fortune and had been treated very well by the local folk as he assembled his kit. He felt, too, that the local Natives had been very supportive and helpful with advice and suggestions for his long trip to the north to strike it rich.

Jim did strike it rich, and when he came back south he stopped at Columbia House again. On his return trip, he hosted a party as a way of saying thanks to all the people who had supported him while he was getting organized here in Edmonton. He wanted to entertain his Native friends, but it was against the law to supply them with any alcoholic beverages. The beverages were readily available to anyone who wanted them, as Jim well knew, but to make it legal he bought a cow, had it butchered, and held a massive barbecue right in the middle of the street in front of the Columbia House. The picture we have shows Jim the following morning, and while Jim may very well have offered nothing stronger than gravy to his Native guests, rumour has it that Jim himself enjoyed the more relaxing liquids available to him.

A lady called Lillian Armstrong Maze has left us a very detailed account of the early years of the Columbia House, and it makes fascinating reading as you look at a chapter of Edmonton history that isn't often recognized.

Another potential prospector, Robert James Armstrong, arrived in Edmonton from Ontario in the spring of 1898, and stayed at the Columbia House. After looking around Edmonton, he decided there was no point in going all the way up to the Klondike. He liked what he saw here, so he sent for his family, settled down, and never really left Edmonton again. Robert Armstrong was Lillian Armstrong Maze's grandfather, and she passes on to us the stories she remembers him telling her.

Nobody seems to know just when the hotel was built. There is a difference of opinion about the name of the original hotel as well. Some records show it as the Big Hotel, others refer to it as the Mammoth Hotel. It appears that the name Columbia House was given to it by a prospector called Jim Gibbons, who was looking for gold in the Columbia River and not having much luck. Somebody called "Flat Boat" McLean was carrying mail to the coast, stopped to talk to Gibbons, and told him of the fortunes to be made panning in the North Saskatchewan at Edmonton. Gibbons came to Edmonton but didn't go panning for gold. He took over the hotel, changed the name to the Columbia House, and made his fortune that way.

Jim Delaney gave Edmontonians a new meaning to the term summer barbecue, and we're still talking about the party he held in front of the Columbia Hotel on his way back from the Klondike.

All of this must have happened around 1890, because we know that in 1891 Gibbons built a small annex to the hotel that he operated as a wholesale liquor outlet. Lease documents tell us that Gibbons rented the hotel in 1893 for $720 a year.

Each room was supplied with pitchers of fresh water every morning, rain water in the summer, melted snow during the winter. The heating system wasn't quite as efficient. On many winter mornings the water in the pitchers would be frozen. The kitchen was well known locally for the quality of the food served. They made their own bread, there was local beef and fowl, and they brought in fish from Lac Ste. Anne.

The local isolation facility for anyone with a communicable disease was known as the pest house. It wasn't really an isolation hospital; it was really a collection of tents tucked into the bush and poplar trees beside the Columbia House. About all you could see of them were the yellow banners that indicated the presence of smallpox. The patients tended to wander around town a little, and our four police officers were often called upon to usher them back to their tents. The little liquor store next to the hotel was a convenient, if not a wise, place to stock up on medicine that could be taken internally to help in the recovery process.

In 1899 the North West Mounted Police took over the building and used it as their headquarters while their permanent home was being built just to the east of the Columbia House.

The Mounties moved in 1900, and the name of the establishment was changed to the Tourist House. With the passage of time the wooden structure deteriorated rather badly. Repairs and renovations enabled it to carry on for a few more years as a rooming house, but that, too, ended with the passage of more years, and the site was later turned into a service station to meet the automotive needs of a changing city. Today it's a parking lot.

The Columbia House address for years was the corner of Jasper Avenue and Grierson Street. It was a small triangle of land that corresponds to Jasper and 101 Avenue in today's terms, but it's a piece of real estate that holds a lot of history and makes a nice home for the ghosts of the Columbia House Hotel.

A Lump of Gold
and a Grain of Salt

You could spend all of your life right here in Edmonton and never know that the area that houses the Valley Zoo and some very nice residences was once known as Miners' Flats. One of the houses that graces this part of town belonged to D. K. Yorath, a successful Edmonton businessman. And that is where our story begins.

According to the telephone directory of the time, the Yorath address was 8302 131 Street. Before Mr. Yorath could start building his house something had to be done about the old stone fireplace that stood in the middle of their new lot. The fireplace was built of stones glued into place with a mortar of mud and straw. The fireplace didn't take kindly to the shift, and resisted every method of transport that tried to move it in one piece.

That fireplace and the term Miners' Flats take us further back into Edmonton history than you might at first suspect, and provide a remarkable story. It's a story of gold and a man who chased it half-way around the world. It's the story of English Charlie, although there are those who claim that some parts of English Charlie's story should be taken with a grain of salt.

English Charlie is more formally known as Charles Stevenson, a London newspaper boy who decided he had best see the rest of the world. He stowed away on a ship sailing for the United States, made it to New York, and went back into the newspaper business, this time selling his papers on the streets of his new home town. In some records English Charlie's last name is spelt Stevenson and in other documents Stephenson.

The year was 1849, and some of the stories printed in the newspapers Charlie was selling told of a gold strike in California. The next we hear of Charlie Stevenson he was in California, panning for gold in the Sacramento Valley. The California placer gold was soon cleaned out, but not before English Charlie managed to fill a baking powder tin with gold nuggets, not just once, but many times over.

English Charlie told the story of his California days to friends in Edmonton, and in the narration he referred to his income from the panned gold. Depending on the size of the baking powder tin, the can full of gold

61

No matter what you've heard about Charlie Stevenson
(and his fireplace), it's probably true. He was a character in
every sense of the word, and he lived down on Miner's Flats.

would bring him between four and eight thousand dollars. This may be where the first grain of salt comes into the picture. When asked how long that tin can full of gold would last when Charlie hit town, he said about four weeks. And there goes another grain of salt.

The word among the California gold miners told of a new field that was just opening up to the north in British Columbia. About 1859, English Charlie made his way to the Cariboo country of British Columbia, but the end of the rainbow was just beyond Charlie's grasp. Again word had it that there was gold to be found along the banks of the North Saskatchewan River and with a fellow prospector, he made his way up through the Okanagan country. About 1876, they crossed the mountains and explored the southern part of what would become Alberta. He panned the South Saskatchewan around Fort Pitt but there wasn't enough gold to make the panning worthwhile. From there Charlie moved north to Edmonton, or Fort Edmonton as it was known at the time, and panned for gold upstream from the fort.

The way Charlie would tell the story to friends as they sat around the campfire, somewhere around Lethbridge a band of Blood Indians stole his pony and gear, leaving him with nothing but a blanket and a rifle. During his wanderings across the flat Alberta prairie, a blizzard caught Charlie by surprise. A herd of buffalo was fleeing the storm, and Charlie shot the biggest animal in the herd. He cleaned out the inside of the animal as best he could, then crawled into it and waited out the storm. This, remember, is Charlie's version of what happened.

Charlie eventually settled on the piece of land that we refer to today as Laurier Heights. The present subdivision gets its name from Sir Wilfrid Laurier, but in the minds of the local people of Charlie's time, it was known as Miners' Flats. Another gold panner had built himself a cabin to the north of Charlie's so the flat land next to the river was bracketed by miners' cabins.

Charlie built his cabin next to the river and was warmed, no doubt, by the fire in his old stone fireplace. In Charlie's later years, legend has it that he spent the winters with Donald Ross and his wife at the Edmonton Hotel, then moved back to his cabin each spring. Charlie had obtained homesteaders rights to the land, and about 1903 a local realtor bought a parcel of the land from Charlie for $12 per acre. The real estate agent was S. H. Smith, and it is his record of English Charlie's adventures that tells us most of what we know of Charlie today.

Mr. Smith tells us that some years later, when he was down on Miners' Flats, he found people living in the old Stevenson cabin, and in conversation with the residents he learned that the man was the grandson of English Charlie.

The cabin burned down a few years later, but the fireplace survived. Every effort was made to move the fireplace to a permanent location, but the mud mortar crumbled, and although the stones were marked by the movers with the thought that the fireplace would be rebuilt, it didn't work. The workmen found an old bent rifle barrel that had been used as a reinforcing rod over the hearth while Charlie was building his fireplace. Along with the legend of English Charlie, there is the riddle of the rifle barrel. Could that have been the rifle that Charlie used to shoot the buffalo that saved his life in the blizzard?

Edmonton's
Field of Dreams

You could probably stump an old Edmonton baseball fan by asking him when you'll find a Ducey that's not a Diamond. The answer, of course, is when they are two separate ball parks.

The baseball field in the Rossdale area of downtown Edmonton has quite a story to tell. The most recent renovations at the ball park replaced a facility that had been in existence since 1933, which makes it long in the tooth for a sporting facility in this city. But a great many Edmontonians don't realize that we've been playing baseball in that part of Edmonton since 1906, but that the game was then being played on a different field.

There is a picture taken in 1952 that you'll find on file down at the City of Edmonton Archives. At first glance you don't realize that it shows Edmonton's baseball history, but take a closer look. In the foreground, as you look down past the towers of the Macdonald Hotel, you notice the fence of a skating rink in the middle of a field. There is a skating shack on the south side of the rink boards, and the makings of a rather basic baseball diamond just to the left of the shack.

In the background and off to the right you can see the playing field that we now know as Telus Field, although it was known as John Ducey Park for a number of years. And those two baseball diamonds just about sum up the history of the game in Edmonton. There are some marvellous ghosts and some wonderful stories hanging around those two fields, spots that really are Edmonton's Field of Dreams.

The field in the foreground was called Diamond Park, and sporting activities certainly weren't limited to baseball. At one time or another, the field has seen games of cricket, rugby, soccer, and lacrosse. In the fall the portion of the field next to the road was flooded, and there was skating and hockey all winter long. Patterns changed, and more and more skating and hockey began taking place in closed arenas. An old die-hard of the Edmonton Parks and Recreation Department, Jack Reilly, wrote to Commissioner John Hodgson, pointing out that the speed skaters in Edmonton had never really had a spot to call their own. Could the commissioner come up with the money to fix up the field for this growing sport? The answer was yes, and Diamond Park added another activity to its long list.

It was around 1906 when the first fence went up around Diamond Park. A man called Frank Gray got things into motion when he made a deal with Donald Ross, who owned the property, for the use of the land. Another small piece of Edmonton's history drops into place.

The early baseball names sound like something out of a Robert Kinsella novel: "Dinny" Maguire, "Chesty" Cox, "Wild Bill" Hurley, Slim "Sunflower" Dell, and "Deacon" White. The Deacon brought a team up from Anacortes, Washington, to play a pick-up Edmonton team on a field up on top of the riverbank, but stuck around to become permanently involved in the Edmonton baseball scene.

George Mackintosh, former sports editor of the *Edmonton Journal*, once wrote about Beans Reardon, who got his start umpiring at Diamond Park and went on to a successful career as an umpire in the National League. George also told of two other umpires who weren't so fortunate. Wheeler and Longnecker were their names, and they didn't call the game the way the Edmonton fans felt it should be called. George pictures them fleeing up the wooden steps to the top of McDougall Drive, closely pursued by a hail of pop bottles hurled by the irate fans.

But then it was 1933, and on May 24, Renfrew Ball Park held its first game. The South Siders played the Royals, and the game got under way at 3:30. We learn from the *Edmonton Bulletin* that the South Siders won 3-0, paced by "the strong seven-hit pitching of Herman Loblick."

But where did the name Renfrew Park come from? In true Edmonton tradition, they held a contest. And true to Edmonton tradition, 450 names were submitted. The winning entry came from a young man named Bunny Moir, who lived at 10630 74 Avenue at the time. He suggested that the ball park be named in honour of Lord Renfrew, and Bunny was the only one who proposed that name. Young Moir got a season pass and $5 for his winning entry.

Lights were added during the summer of 1947, and the newspapers told us that the floodlights made Renfrew one of the most up-to-date sports stadiums in western Canada.

Over the baseball years in Edmonton, the name John Ducey is mentioned most of all. He had organized a baseball team at the age of eleven, when the altar boys at St. Anthony's parish challenged the boys at St. Joseph's. Young John not only played ball for the St. Joseph's team, but managed it as well. His interest in the sport never flagged over the years, and in September 1983, when John Ducey passed away at the age of seventy-five, it was decided to rename Renfrew Park in his honour. That name change did take place but not without some controversy. There were those who felt that Renfrew was an old and honourable name, and should not be changed. There were others who felt that something else should be named in Mr. Baseball's honour. But the Ducey's fans won out.

It's a little spooky to discover, too, that the ball park is built on the site of Edmonton's first cemeteries. The white settlers' cemetery and the nearby Native burial ground have turned up evidence of the site's earlier use over the years. They were in use from the early 1800s to about 1880.

All of which makes it even more interesting as we look forward to the old familiar shout from Edmonton's Field of Dreams: "Play ball!"

We took our fairs, exhibitions, and sports seriously in early Edmonton and built a splendid facility down on the Ross Flats area to host them.

A Sad Story in Strathcona

The fire started on Saturday night, June 8, 1907. Before it was extinguished, five workers had died in the fire and another, the next day in hospital. Strathcona reeled from the tragedy that took place in a coal mine just east of the High Level Bridge.

The mine was owned and operated by John Walter. When the Walter name comes up, we think in terms of York boats, cable ferries, lumber mills, and steamboats. John Walter played a part in all of these ventures and was a success in each of them. But his coal-mining venture nearly shattered his self-confidence. He was deeply moved by the events that took the lives of the men.

John Walter was one of the real old-timers. He came here in 1870 to build York boats for the Hudson's Bay Company. He worked out his five-year contract and stayed right here and made his fortune. There are a great many firsts attributed to John. He was the first person to settle across the river from the fort. That would have made him the first south-sider. He was the first Edmonton businessman to make his fortune here. He brought in a reel of cable by cart from Winnipeg, strung it across the river, and established the first cable ferry here in 1882. Up to that point, if you wanted to cross the river you forded it, and the chances are you were lucky if only your feet got wet.

John brought the first cook stove to Edmonton, again by cart from Winnipeg. He built the sternwheeler *The City of Edmonton*. During the week he used it as a work boat to bring lumber downstream for his Edmonton mills, and for the weekends he fitted it with a dance floor on the top deck and sailed it as an excursion boat, taking up to five hundred passengers on runs upstream to Big Island and back.

Around 1880 he tried his hand at operating a general store, and twice he saw his lumber mills, and his fortune, wiped out by flooding in the North Saskatchewan. The first flood in 1899 was bad, and the second in 1915 brought even more financial difficulties to John Walter.

But floods and financial setbacks didn't bother him as much as the fire in his coal mine, and the lives lost in that blaze. John Walter had tried the coal-mining business twice, and neither venture was very successful. It was at the second mine that the tragic fire hit on that June night.

The mine was on the south side of the river, just below the top of the bank and just east of where the High Level Bridge sits today, roughly at 108 Street. Just a little before midnight that Saturday, a fire broke out at the entrance to the mine. There were five men on the night shift, all working inside the mine. The foreman that night was George Lamb, who had spotted the fire, sounded the alarm, and knowing that the crew was working below, headed down the shaft to warn them. There were actually three passages out of the mine, but all were sealed off by the fire and there was no way the trapped miners could escape. Lamb tried to make his way through the flames to the lower entrance of the mine, but when he reached the outside air, his clothing was on fire. He got as far as the engine house, which was also in flames, then collapsed and was taken to hospital.

George Lamb died in hospital the next day. The other five miners never made it out of the bottom of the shaft. Funeral services for the six victims were held on the same day and at the same time.

The five Protestants were buried from Wainwright's Undertaking Parlour on Whyte Avenue and 104 Street. There were so many people who wanted to pay their respects that Wainwright's built a special platform outside their business premises and Reverend W. R. George performed the services from there. The funeral for the sixth man was held at St. Anthony's Roman Catholic Church just to the west along Whyte Avenue. The businessmen of Strathcona closed their operations during the services, and the funerals were timed so that the two processions made their way to the cemeteries at the same time. There was a procession a mile long that followed the bodies to the cemeteries, with the churches of Strathcona slowly pealing their bells as the caskets made their way through the town.

John and his wife, Annie, had lived through some difficult times. There had been the flood in 1899 when their house survived but the lumber mill was washed away by the flooding river. Then in 1915 another flood hit, this time with a crest four feet higher than the one in 1899, and again John Walter saw his lumber mill swept away. But that fire was the worst.

Five years after the last flood, and just before Christmas, Annie Walter saw her husband taken to the Royal Alex Hospital. She waited as he underwent surgery on December 23. And she spent Christmas Day, 1920, trying to sort out how she was going to survive the death of her husband earlier that morning in the hospital.

*He came to build York boats for the Hudson's Bay Company and
stayed to build a legend for himself, for his family, and for Edmonton.
He was John Walter, the Orkney entrepreneur, pictured here in 1899
with his wife Annie and their two sons, John W. and Stanley.*

John Walter was deemed to be a kind man, a good employer, and an honest citizen of this town. And while the story of the Orkney boat builder who came to our community in 1870 and died here fifty years later is the story of a successful husband, father, and businessman, there were some sad chapters in the tale. The fire in his coal mine that June night many years ago was one of them.

The Arrival
of the Cars

When it's the Friday evening rush hour, you're running late, and the Whitemud Freeway is a long thin parking lot because somebody tail-ended a truck at the off-ramp at Fox Drive, you can't help thinking that automobiles and Alberta have been going steady since the dawn of time.

Although that's not true, cars did arrive in Alberta a long time ago. And the story makes for an interesting chapter in our city's history. If you're driving south on 109 Street and passing University Avenue, you may notice a small park on the east side of the street. It's called Joe Morris Park, and you may not have given much thought to just who Joe Morris might be. He was the gentleman who brought the first automobile to the city of Edmonton, and that's why he is recognized with his own park.

Bob Edwards of *Calgary Eye Opener* fame once said that the first thing a man with an automobile runs into is debt. Bob documented a great many things while he dispensed his personal philosophy in the pages of his newspaper. He said, in an issue on August 8, 1902, "Billy Cochrane of High River has introduced the first automobile into Alberta. High River is the pioneer of progress. Okotoks still clings to the Red River cart."

It should be noted that Bob Edwards was living in High River at the time, and always a local booster, there was no way he was going to miss a chance to poke fun at the rival community of Okotoks when the opportunity presented itself. Remember, too, that Bob Edwards started his paper in High River, and called it the *Eye Opener* because he felt everyone should have one.

By 1904 Edwards had moved himself and his paper to Calgary, where he reported on the second automobile to arrive in Alberta, a gasoline-burning Rambler owned by John Prince. It calls for a little checking of dates here to see who was second into the automobile business in Alberta, because on May 25, 1904, Edmonton's Joe Morris drove his car from the south side down Scona Hill, over the Low Level Bridge, up McDougall Hill, and down Jasper Avenue. Joe's car, by the way, was a Ford, and Cochrane's car in High River was a Stanley Steamer.

71

The *Edmonton Bulletin* reported the arrival of the first car in the city in their issue of May 26, 1904, noting that: "The credit of bringing the first horseless carriage to Edmonton belongs to Mr. J. H. Morris, who, on his return from Winnipeg last evening, brought a two-cylinder autocar. The new carriage created quite an excitement on Jasper Avenue last evening, especially among the horses and small boys."

Credit for bringing the first car to the province may go to the south, but we can take credit for another part of the Alberta automotive saga. In his book *A History of Alberta*, Jim MacGregor tells us that it was an Edmonton dealer who sold a car to a Calgary buyer, and then delivered it. That makes it the first recorded car trip between Edmonton and Calgary, and that happened early in March 1906. MacGregor, in his marvellous book, documents the trip with a quote from the *Edmonton Bulletin* of March 2, 1906:

> The party left Edmonton on Saturday morning at ten, and arrived in Calgary at seven on Sunday evening, staying in Red Deer over Saturday night. From Lacombe to Red Deer, 20 miles, the car made the trip in 34 minutes. During the trip, 20 gallons of gasoline were used and one gallon of lubricating oil.

That car was a twenty-nine horsepower four-seater, bought by W. H. White of Calgary. The super-salesman at the Edmonton end was G. Carriveau. The gas consumption for a twenty-nine horsepower motor was bad enough, but a gallon of oil? Maybe they pulled into Red Deer and said, "Fill it up with oil and check the gas."

Another interesting piece in Jim MacGregor's book has to do with the governance of motor vehicle traffic in the province. It was on April 23, 1906, that J. R. Boyle, the MLA for Sturgeon, moved "An Act to Regulate the Speed and Operation of Motor Vehicles on Highways."

You had to register your car with the provincial secretary and take out a permit. You were given a number and a licence and had to carry the number with you when driving, and it had to be in plain sight. You also had to carry lights if you were driving at night.

That act makes interesting reading in terms of today's speed limits. Maximum speed was to be twenty miles per hour in the country, except when you were overtaking a horse-drawn vehicle—then you had to slow down to ten miles per hour. If you were meeting a rig coming towards you, speed was to be reduced to five miles per hour, but if the horses were frightened and looked as though they were getting out of control, you were to stop. In a city, town, or incorporated village, the maximum speed was to be ten miles per hour. And unless he could prove that he had taken every reasonable precaution to prevent it, a driver was held responsible if he frightened a horse.

And that, probably, is another reason why they are referred to as the Good Old Days. Parking meters, on the other hand, didn't appear on Edmonton streets until the summer of 1948, and when first introduced, you got a full hour for a nickel, and a penny bought you twelve minutes of parking time. Imagine that.

Meet Joe Morris (driver), the man who brought the automobile to Edmonton and drove it down Jasper Avenue, to the delight of small boys and the distress of large horses.

A Fire Hall that's
Not a Fire Hall

When is a fire hall not a fire hall? When it's a furniture store or a theatre. All of which is true of the No. 6 Fire Station that has stood, relatively firm and strong, on 83 Avenue and 104 Street since 1910. It has changed uses over the years, but the history of the structure and the charm of its story are still solid today.

There are a number of photographs of the south side fire hall, one of which shows the Strathcona Fire Brigade in 1901. The picture shows the horse-drawn rig and a collection of men in civilian clothes grouped in front of the open doors of the hall. A little reading reveals that this was the Strathcona Volunteer Fire Brigade, and in addition to the fire fighters, everybody who was somebody on the south side came over to the fire hall to get into the picture. There was the editor of the *Strathcona Plain Dealer*, the pharmacist, the jeweller, the manager of the new Edmonton Brewery, and the man who ran the hardware store. A. E. Tighe took the photograph, although it ended up in the Ernest Brown collection.

There are a lot of other photographs of the south side fire hall, but there is something different about them. Then you notice the doorways. In the 1901 picture there are no white keystones over the arches. Are they the same fire halls at all?

The answer is no, they are not the same building. The 1901 photo shows the original south side hall. The 1901 building was erected the year the picture was taken, and shows the two-door fire hall that was built to house the Strathcona Volunteer Fire Brigade. The interesting part of the story of the original building is that the firemen found it too cold and unsanitary to live in, and the construction of a new hall began in 1909. The new building was close to the original, but not on the same site.

Wilson and Herrald were the local architects, and they seem to have run into some difficulties while building the new hall. There was a structural crack in one wall that had to be repaired before the building could be occupied, so the completion date shows as 1910.

This new fire hall, when it was finished, was known as Strathcona Fire

Edmonton was a community of wooden buildings, and we constantly lived with the threat of fire, but our courageous fire fighters were always ready to help when the firebell rang.

Hall No. 1. The amalgamation of Strathcona and Edmonton took place two years later, and the Strathcona Fire Department became part of the Edmonton Fire Department, and the building on 83 Avenue became known as Fire Hall No. 6.

The years flew by, and Edmontonians decided, around 1934, that it was time for a new Fire Hall No. 6, so they built it across the street from the old one.

Today, as soon as somebody moves out of an old building, historic old building or not, we tear it down and put up something that's all glass, brass, and smoky mirrors. This wasn't the case in 1934, though, and thank goodness for that. The old Fire Hall No. 6 became the home of Strathcona Furniture. The old No. 6 hall served as Strathcona Furniture's warehouse for twenty years before they had to move out in 1974. The old building had gone downhill rather badly during the two decades it had served the furniture store, and some tough decisions had to be made.

But there was in Edmonton a theatre group called the Walterdale Theatre. It began as an amateur theatre group in an old building in

Walterdale, just south of the bridge and close to where the Kinsmen Field House was built. The group later moved into an old building across the street from the Northern Alberta Institute of Technology, but in 1974 it was looking for a new home. A deal was struck between the City and Walterdale Playhouse, and under the terms of the new lease agreement Walterdale took over the Fire Hall on the provision that the theatre group restore it, and that's what happened.

Many of the original elements of the building were retained. There is a hose tower, eleven feet square and seventy-seven feet high, which tops the building. That's where the hoses were originally hung to dry after they had been used at a fire. The tower also housed the original Strathcona fire bell that was rung to summon the volunteers when a blaze broke out and their services were required.

In the restoration process, the exterior of the building was brought back to the way it looked around 1912, and the interior was adapted for theatre use. The second floor, at one time, contained an office and a bedroom for the fire chief. There was also a fireman's band room, a general room, and five bedrooms for the firemen, and showers in the bathroom.

But what would an old fire hall be without a brass pole for the firemen to slide down when they were on their way to a blaze? Let the record show that the old No. 6 hall had not one, but *two* brass poles. Alberta Culture declared the old building a historic site in 1975. It was noted that it was the oldest fire hall of its vintage in either Edmonton or Calgary.

So the next time you're at the Strathcona Farmer's Market on a Saturday morning, say hello to the Walterdale Playhouse as you go by. The building has quite a history.

Saying It
with Flowers

It's always fun to look through a list of Edmonton firsts: the first car, the first phone call, etc. And then there is the first florist. His name was Walter Ramsay, and the operation he began in 1905 was not only Edmonton's first commercial florist business but was also the first commercial greenhouse operation in northern Alberta. By 1921 it was the largest operation of its kind this far north in Canada.

Nothing underlines the changes that have taken place in Edmonton quite like an old photograph. There is one picture, found in a 1914 pictorial presentation of the city, which makes you wonder at the size of the greenhouse in the photograph. When you look a little closer you realize that the greenhouse is right beside the General Hospital, and in today's terms, it's impossible to imagine a greenhouse that big in that part of town. This was Walter Ramsay's greenhouse in 1914, making his story even more interesting because it was located on the northeast corner of 100 Avenue at 111 Street.

And what is also surprising is that Walter Ramsay wasn't trained to be a florist at all. He was trained to be a schoolteacher, and that's what first brought him to Edmonton.

He was born near London, Ontario, and came to Edmonton in 1899 to teach school in the Clover Bar district. A year later he continued his teaching career in Edmonton and was appointed principal at McKay Avenue School in 1901. That year, along with Walter Ramsay, there were 2,626 people living here.

He was appointed the first principal of the new Queen's Avenue School when it opened in 1903. And what kind of a man was this early school principal? He was the kind of man who never lost his interest in education, and who later, long after he had retired as a classroom teacher and administrator, continued to serve his community as a public school trustee. You might be interested to learn that it was Trustee Walter Ramsay who fought for the right of women to attend evening classes, as well as classes in plumbing and electricity at that. And he did make that happen, in 1917.

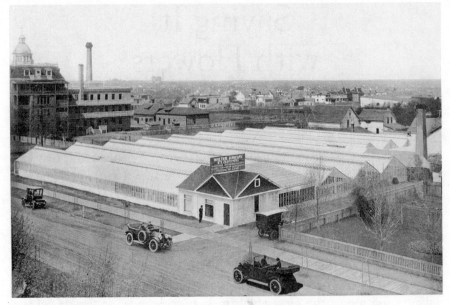

Walter Ramsay came to Edmonton to teach our students, and ended up teaching the whole city how to "say it with flowers" from his greenhouse on Victoria Avenue, shown here in 1914.

All the years that he taught school, he used gardening as a way to relax. He had a home in what is now downtown Edmonton that became a showplace. People were always surprised at what you could grow this far north, and Walter was an experimenter.

We may never know if any one thing triggered his decision, but in 1905 he resigned from the Edmonton Public School Board and began his florist operation. "He always wanted a greenhouse, so he chucked his job and went into business," was the comment made when the replica of Walter's first greenhouse, the one near the General Hospital, was opened down at Fort Edmonton Park.

That original greenhouse mushroomed, and by 1907 there were five structures that covered almost an acre of ground. By 1921, Edmonton's first florist was selling over 170,000 blossoms a year. A news story in the *Edmonton Bulletin* on March 25, 1921, tells us that while Ramsay grew practically all kinds of cut flowers, he specialized in roses and carnations. There were five varieties of roses grown and three kinds of carnations.

The prose of the time was almost as colourful as Walter Ramsay's roses. Another news story dealt, in part, with "A Strong Man's Flower."

New flowers are sometimes very appropriately named, and just as one would expect the "Estelle" carnation to be a saucy, scarlet, piquant little flower, the President Roosevelt carnation should surely have some individuality.

And it has. It is assuredly a strong man's flower. Compact, restrained in outline, but in colour a strong, deep red that warms the air by its very presence there. It hints of passion and control, and is in every way more likely to fit the name of this strenuous president than any white flower of peace.

All that about something you stuck in the buttonhole of your jacket.

On April 13, 1911, Ramsay's was running comparatively large advertisements in the paper, and the prices are interesting. Easter lily plants ran from 75¢ to $2.50. Hydrangeas were $1.50 to $2.50, and hyacinths ran from 25¢ to $1.99. Those were the prices for the plants. Cut flowers were 75¢ per dozen for tulips; daffodils were a dollar a dozen, and a dozen carnations would have cost you $1.50. In 1911 their address was Victoria Avenue at 11 Street and their phone number was 1292.

This grand old gentleman who brought so much colour to the city of his choice passed away just before Christmas in 1958, following a lengthy illness. He was eighty-eight years old.

Walter Ramsay: teacher, florist, businessman, Edmontonian.

Reed's China & Gift Shop

A skill-testing question in 1985 would have caught most Edmontonians without an answer. Given that the Hudson's Bay Company was the oldest retail business in continuous operation in Edmonton, what was the *second* oldest retail business operation in town? Give up? Reed's China & Gift Shop, and the story behind the two men that made this remarkable story possible is a happy one.

It was 1905, and William Henry Reed and Russell F. Clarke came to Edmonton from Belleville, Ontario, to make their fortune. From the day they opened their doors for business, they demonstrated merchandising techniques and sound business practices that are valid even today, but not often found in our high-tech world.

Reed and his brother-in-law Clarke opened a store on Jasper Avenue at 102 Street. By that time Edmonton had been a town in the formal sense for thirteen years. The population was hovering around the eleven thousand mark, and Jasper Avenue, when it rained, was a sea of mud. Wooden sidewalks on both sides of the street made it possible for pedestrians to get around, but in very many ways, life was very basic by today's standards.

The area was doing well, though, because there were always plenty of homesteaders coming to Edmonton and stocking up on those things that they would need to operate their farms. Reed and Clarke set about meeting those needs. They dealt in the basic merchandise required to set up and operate a homestead, but they also sold teas and coffees along with the washtubs and stoves. Reed had earlier managed a store called Stroud's in Belleville, and it's interesting to note that Stroud's was known as the tea king of eastern Ontario. Reed knew his product, and he brought that knowledge to Edmonton. Note, too, that one of the many firsts that they brought to Edmonton was a hand-cranked coffee roaster. Just imagine what the smell of freshly roasted coffee beans did for the shopper when he came in out of the winter cold and into the warmth of the Reed's store before Christmas in 1905.

And it was winter when the store first opened. The two men arrived in

October of 1905, picked out the location of their choice, and opened up for business on November 25, 1905, just one month before Christmas. They leased space in the Lee Block, a wooden structure at the corner of Jasper Avenue and 102 Street. There is something eerie about looking at the pictures of the store that you'll find at the City of Edmonton Archives. You have the definite feeling that you've seen this building, and not all that long ago. This can't be, you think. And then you realize what it is. The original building of Reed's store has been duplicated at Fort Edmonton Park, and so accurately that the building in the park looks just like the one in the old photos.

The store owners stayed at least two jumps ahead of the demands of the local shoppers. They continued to carry the pots, pans, and crockery that homesteaders needed, but they also began to introduce fine china, cut glass, and silverware. There was a growing sophistication to be found on the Edmonton social scene, and Reed's was the only place in town where you could shop for the finer things you needed to grace your table for a proper afternoon tea or a dinner party.

Mr. Reed reached back into the skills he had acquired at Stroud's and experimented with teas and coffees that worked best with the Edmonton water. How's that for anticipating consumer demand?

Alberta became a province on September 1, 1905. G. H. V. Bulyea became our first lieutenant-governor. And when he and Mrs. Bulyea were entertaining at Government House, guess where they bought their teas and coffees, along with their china, cups, saucers, and silverware? If these things were good enough for the lieutenant-governor, surely they were good enough for Edmonton's leading hostesses.

Coffee grinders adding to the bouquet of the store, blending teas to suit the local water, and even the introduction of Edmonton's first Santa Claus parade are attributed to the two men behind Reed's China & Gift Shop. All these innovations, with Santa travelling along Jasper Avenue in a rig pulled by a team of horses, then visiting the city schools at recess to hand out gifts to the kids, and later the introduction of Edmonton's first year-round toy department, came from these two men. They were merchandisers; there can be no question about that. They also happened to introduce the city's first bridal registry in the 1920s.

The start of the story is documented in the fine penmanship of Mr. Reed, beginning with the day they opened for business in 1905: "W. H. Reed this day commences business. Cash in bank $522.40. Cash in Till $50.00. Cash sales $140.00."

In the weeks that followed business wasn't always that good. There were weeks when sales totalled only $9.00, or in another instance, $27.50.

But they survived and prospered, and proudly served Edmontonians. In 1913 Reed's opened a second store in the Blowey-Henry Building at the east end of Jasper Avenue because the Pantages Theatre people had acquired the Lee Building that housed the original store. Pantages wanted to add an extension to the theatre they had under construction next door, the venue that became the Strand in later years. But the Lee Building caught fire on January 11 and was then demolished. Reed's carried on business in the Blowey-Henry location, calling it Reed's Bazaar, then moved back to the west end of Jasper Avenue in 1917. In 1927 they relocated again, this time next door to 10325 Jasper Avenue, and changed their name back to Reed's China & Gift Shop. In 1985 they celebrated their eightieth birthday, and by then had grown to a series of outlets around the city.

Reed's China & Gift Shop: a success story, yes, but also a people story in every sense.

In the early years, it was Reed's China & Gift Shop that enabled Edmontonians to enjoy the likes of fine china, cutlery, pleasant teas, and rich coffees in their western homes.

It Takes a Y's Man

It was a cold winter's day in 1906 when the Young Men's Christian Association (YMCA) opened its doors in Edmonton, and the organization has been making a difference ever since.

It was February 6, 1908, when the building that looks so familiar to us today was formally opened. It looks familiar because it really hasn't changed much over the years. Added to, yes, but the original building is still recognizable.

They began talking about building a YMCA in Edmonton away back in 1903. That's even before we incorporated as a city. The population was already creeping up to the eight thousand mark. The first meeting was held four days before Christmas. About all we know of the discussions is that they decided to form a committee to look into the possibility of creating a YMCA here in Edmonton. On January 4, just after Christmas, they started raising funds, and, through a great deal of hard work raised enough money to put up the original structure.

They laid the cornerstone for the new building on July 1, 1907, and it was quite an event. It was perhaps fitting that they got a lady involved. They asked the wife of Alberta's first lieutenant-governor, Mrs. Bulyea, to do the honours, and she did it with style. She used a silver trowel, which she tapped against the cornerstone, and said in a loud, clear voice, "I declare to be well and truly laid, this, the cornerstone of the Young Men's Christian Association of Edmonton."

And what they tucked in under the cornerstone showed a lot of imagination, too. They picked up a tin box that they filled with things that told the story of Edmonton in 1907. There were some coins in the box, of course. The coins had the portrait of the reigning monarch on one side— Edward VII it was at the time—and they also put in a few newspapers. We had three newspapers in Edmonton in 1907, the *Edmonton Journal*, morning and evening editions, the *Daily Bulletin*, and the *Saturday News*. All three papers were represented under that cornerstone.

The news stories catch you a little by surprise. There was talk of the new bridge that was in the planning stage. They thought they would call it the High Level Bridge, and the feeling was that the south end of it would be somewhere near the University of Alberta campus. All this was adding fuel to an already inflated real estate market. Some of the other stories in the papers of the day whispered of the possible merger of the two cities, Edmonton on the north side of the river and Strathcona on the south.

You would be hard pressed to come up with the name of the first man to join the Edmonton YMCA, but if anyone asks, you can say that he was Mr. Percy Williams. Mr. Williams signed up on November 17, 1907, but unfortunately didn't get a chance to use his membership much because he moved to Denver, Colorado, on November 18, 1907. But it takes a Y's man to hang onto a membership card. Percy Williams came back to Edmonton on September 17, 1962, went to the Y, and produced his membership card. He was treated royally, of course, and Mr. Williams then carried on with his trip to Salmon Arm, BC.

There were 474 members when the building opened on that February day in 1908. The following year it jumped up to 712, and a newspaper story that ran on October 12, 1910, reported that there were 1,009 members as of the end of April of that year. The first full-time secretary, Mr. R. B. Chadwick, arrived in Edmonton to take over the new operation on April 5, 1906.

The YMCA, seen here in 1911, has been a part of Edmonton since 1907 when the wife of our first lieutenant-governor laid the cornerstone for the very building that still houses the downtown YMCA today.

The Y was taking off all across Canada. There were new buildings going up in Halifax, Sherbrooke, Montreal, Oshawa, Hamilton, Owen Sound, Woodstock, Collingwood, Orillia, Kenora, Regina, Calgary, Lethbridge, Revelstoke, Victoria, and, of course, here in Edmonton.

There was another nice touch of Edmonton history in the stories that ran at the time the building was completed. We had street names, not numbers, and if you were describing the location of the Y you could say that it was on May Street, at the head of Howard Avenue.

There was a major four-storey addition completed in 1951. They brought in the current lieutenant-governor, J. J. Bowlen, to do the honour this time, but we don't know whether he had a silver trowel or not. We do know, though, that they put the new cornerstone right on top of the old one.

Shortly after the Edmonton Y opened, they produced a small booklet that talked of the benefits of membership. That booklet makes interesting reading today. The recommended clothing for boys in the gymnasium was a "black quarter-sleeve vest with a triangle of yellow braid, with 8 inch sides and the letter E in the centre."

The booklet described, in detail, what the Y would do for you. If you participated in the exercises and games in the YMCA gymnasium, "It will strengthen the weak, straighten the bent, fatten the thin and make all healthy and strong and courageous."

And you can't ask much more than that of any organization.

What,
No Air Miles Points?

In a recent issue of the *Edmonton Journal* there was an article about the downtown farmer's market. It made for interesting reading, and it certainly made you realize that how people buy groceries has changed over the years.

A visit to the farmer's market was a Saturday thing. Of course, over the years Edmontonians have had to pick up their food requirements during the week as well. And there were many items you needed that they didn't carry at the farmer's market: soap, breakfast cereal, canned pork and beans—things like that.

That's where the corner store came into the picture. Early Edmonton neighbourhoods always had a corner store. The owners lived in the back of the shop, and if your mother discovered that she had run out of salt for the morning porridge, a small child would be dispatched to the corner store to get some. The porridge had to be made the night before and cooked in a double boiler over the pilot light on the stove all night. The fact that the store was closed didn't make any difference. The lights were on at the back, so you hammered on the door, told the shopkeeper your problem, and he brought you the salt.

Then there was the delivery element. To be one up on the competition, the corner-store owners realized that they had to offer extra services. One of those services was delivery of your groceries. You picked them out by pointing to the items on the shelves behind the owner or his wife. Then they were piled up on the counter, and, after they had been paid for, they were carefully placed in a used cardboard box. Your name was printed on the outside with a black wax pencil, and after school that day some enterprising young fellow with a double-bar CCM bicycle with a grocery rack on the front pedalled his way from school to the store. He spent the next couple of hours delivering the boxes to the waiting housewives.

Then the grocery business began to grow and diversify. Presumably it was all done in the name of progress. On the north side of 111 Avenue just east of 95 Street a gentleman named Harry Tait opened an outlet bigger than your usual corner store. He chose a fancy name for it, too. He called it Harry Tait's Groceteria, and the name seemed to catch on. Your average corner store carried just about everything that your needs might dictate, but Harry Tait gave you a wider selection of brands.

The groceteria concept grew, and Harry Tait soon had other stores around town, including one on 124 Street near 102 Avenue. But the major department stores in the downtown area were not about to be left out of all of this.

Eaton's soon had a grocery department, as did The Bay. And of course Woodward's had a department that they called their Groceteria. The big stores took Harry Tait's idea and carried it one step further. They had even more brands and sizes from which to choose, but they kept the corner store concept as well. All of the big department stores delivered their customers' purchases. The lady of the house usually carried out the grocery shopping, and she made her way to the downtown area by either bus or streetcar. There was no way she was going to lug boxes of heavy groceries home on the bus, and nobody had a car. That left the delivery function to be carried out by the stores, and they did, sometimes for a fee, but not always.

There is a picture on file at the City of Edmonton Archives that shows the interior of the Eaton's grocery department before the store opened. The picture was taken June 27, 1951, and there isn't a customer in sight. It has to have been taken before the store opened because the shelves are all neatly stacked, and there isn't a can of beans out of line.

You can see the wire shopping carts that were provided for the use of the customers, but even they look a little different than they do today. They were smaller for one thing, they didn't have the drop seat for the child accompanying mom, and you didn't have to plug a 25¢ piece into a coin slot before you tried to unlock it from the sixteen carts it was rammed into. There was no admonishment about taking the cart off the parking lot, because there was no parking lot. The grocery department at Eaton's was downstairs, and you'd simply never have made it up the escalator with it.

In the foreground of this picture you can see three cardboard boxes, one on top of the other, with the top one open. A good magnifying glass helps us see that the boxes contained Perky dog and cat food. Imagine! Feeding a dog and a cat the same pet food! In any self-respecting superstore these days, the pets have an aisle all to themselves, with the dog food on one side and the cat food on the other, and never the twain shall meet.

A look at the shelves and the products reminds you that each item had a price marked on it. With a good clerk on the check-out stand, the only time you're really conscious of the price of an item these days is when the scanner doesn't pick up the bar code and the clerk has to swipe it three times over the red light.

The products offered for sale in today's grocery store have changed as well. Nowadays your average super outlet offers more kinds of motor oil than there were kinds of soup in Eaton's in 1951. It seems that the only thing you can't find are used motorcycle parts.

But through it all there are still the farmer's markets operating here in Edmonton. They carry a touch of the way we were, and a Saturday morning visit to the Old Strathcona Farmer's Market is a joy. You're all right as long as you don't make eye contact with Otto, the sausage man. If you do, you come home with $5 worth of pepperoni that you hadn't intended to buy, but you will enjoy every bite.

Today we call them convenience stores, but past generations of Edmontonians called them corner stores. They were an integral part of every neighborhood.

Welcome to
Edmonton

I t was on March 15, 1906, that the first sitting of the newly created
Province of Alberta's Legislative Assembly took place in Edmonton. This
is a very interesting part of our city's history, but what makes the event
uniquely Edmontonian is that the sitting took place in a hockey arena just
four days after the last game of the season had been played.

The venue for our Legislative Assembly representatives was the Thistle
Rink, a huge building on the east side of 102 Street just north of Jasper
Avenue. It was probably chosen because of its size. It was the largest
enclosed building west of Winnipeg at the time, measuring over two hundred feet in length and over eighty feet in width.

Edmonton entrepreneur Richard Secord built the Thistle Rink in 1902.
Secord believed in Edmonton and its future, and acted accordingly. His
confidence in Edmonton really paid off for him, and the Thistle Rink was
just one of the investments he made in his town that became a municipal
focal point.

The Thistle Rink was the scene of many major events in our city's history. During that first legislative session, newspaper reports claimed that
four thousand people had jammed the Thistle to hear Lieutenant-Governor
Bulyea read the first speech from the Throne. Technically, the capacity of
the rink was less than half that, but Edmontonians take their politics seriously, and it's distinctly possible that there were that many of the faithful in
attendance.

The Thistle was also the scene of the Inaugural Ball that was held to
mark the creation of the Province of Alberta. That all happened on
September 1, 1905, making it another big day in Edmonton's history.

The political situation at the time was such that under Prime Minister
Wilfrid Laurier, Clifford Sifton, as minister of the Interior, had introduced
an immigration policy that had done great things for the west and paved
the way for the creation of our new province. When Sifton resigned,
Laurier named an Edmontonian to take his place—and it wasn't just any
Edmontonian, either. It was a gentleman named Frank Oliver. To state that

*Only in Edmonton would they scrape the ice out of an old
hockey arena, the Thistle Rink, and set up chairs for the first
sitting of the newly created Alberta Legislature in 1905.*

Oliver was an Edmonton booster would be the understatement of the decade. Frank Oliver gets credit for seeing to it that Edmonton was named the temporary capital of the new province in 1905, and he probably played no small part in making sure that it was named the permanent capital in 1906. You might be interested in knowing that Calgary, Red Deer, and Banff, among other centres, were in the running for the honour of being named the provincial capital.

Marking that first sitting of the Alberta Legislative Assembly is a photograph of the event. For this we are indebted to Cassell Tait, a highly talented Edmonton photographer. You have to remember, too, that in 1905 the art of photography was in good hands, but the technology was far removed from what it is today. The picture that Tait took would have been a time exposure, and how he lit that huge space and got the participants to hold still while the shutter was open we can only guess. Looking at a print of that picture you can't help but be impressed with the changes that were brought about by some bunting and a few flags. That night, after the legislative sitting, they cleaned all the seats out of the way and held a dance. Walter Clarke and his ten-piece orchestra provided the music.

Cassell Tait has left us a great photographic record of the Inauguration Ceremony on September 1, 1905, as well. We had all the national figures right here in our city on that occasion. Sir Wilfrid Laurier and Lady Laurier were here, as was Governor General Earl Grey, Lieutenant-Governor Bulyea, and all the local celebrities. The day got underway with a parade that began outside the Immigration Hall on 96 Street and Jasper, worked its way west along Jasper, then down 102 Street and the hill to Robs Flats, about where the new baseball park was being built. The parade was timed to arrive there just before noon, because that's when the big event was to take place. Bulyea signed the register of the crown on a huge, raised platform, and became our first lieutenant-governor. After this ceremony came the reading of the King's Proclamation, and Alberta was a province. It all happened at high noon that day, and again there was a major dance at the Thistle Rink that night, with Walter Clarke and his group providing the music once more.

But the Thistle has one more claim to political fame—it was the scene of the first documented political joke in local history. On September 1, 1905, when Alberta had become a province, the sitting member for Strathcona in the North-West Territories Legislative Assembly, A. C. Rutherford, was named premier of the new province. After he had been called upon to form a government, Rutherford did some fast organizing and called an election for November 9, 1905.

In Edmonton, W. A. Griesbach was running against a formidable opponent, Charlie Cross. Frank Oliver gave a ringing speech in support of his friend Charlie. When Griesbach stood up to make his pitch, he said that, after facing the formidable force of a Frank Oliver speech, he felt a little like David facing Goliath. Frank Oliver rose in rebuttal, and said that he was surprised that Griesbach, instead of using the weapon with which David slew Goliath, had chosen instead to use the weapon Samson had used so destructively on the Philistines—the jawbone of an ass. We note in passing that Charlie Cross was elected, and decisively, but of course the war of words had nothing to do with it.

That great landmark of Edmonton history, the Thistle Rink, caught fire and burned to the ground on October 31, 1913.

A Salute to the King Edward

If you stand across the street from Manulife Place and close your eyes a little, you will probably see the ghost of the King Edward Hotel in the shadows of the newer structure.

It was back in 1905 and 1906 when two Edmonton businessmen decided that what the city needed was a first-class hotel. The names of the two gentlemen were Jack Calhoun and R. Ferguson, and they had been doing business at the corner of 101 Street and 102 Avenue for years. They didn't call it 102 Avenue, though—to them it was Athabasca Avenue. We liked naming avenues after Canadian rivers in those years. Athabasca is now 102 Avenue, Peace is now 103 Avenue, Nelson is now 107 Avenue, and if you want to get extra fancy, 114 Avenue was Stikeen and 113 Avenue was Brazeau. All that changed in 1914 when we adopted the numbering system, but that didn't affect Calhoun and Ferguson until long after they had opened their hotel.

Before they built their hotel they were in the business of supplying miners and prospectors with their outfits, and they did very well at it. When they built the hotel, they named it after the reigning monarch of the day, King Edward. It opened in November of 1906.

They were situated just a couple of blocks south of the CNR Station and business was splendid. It was so good that they decided to expand the hotel, and to do so they sold off some of the last of their land to the south of the King Edward. They were just using the land for corrals at the time anyway, in connection with their old outfitting business, and they really needed the extra space and capital. This addition was completed in 1910 and more than doubled the capacity of the King Edward to 110 rooms.

There had been other hotels in Edmonton down through the years. Donald Ross opened the Edmonton Hotel in the late 1870s. He didn't really open a hotel. It more or less emerged from the need for a place for people to stay until they got settled in the new community, so he opened his home, for a fee, and looked after them. Then there was Luke Kelly's Saloon that grew into the wooden Alberta Hotel, which later grew into the brick

Alberta Hotel. But for sheer class, you couldn't beat the King Edward, until the Hotel Macdonald opened in 1915.

All the visiting dignitaries stayed at the King Edward, including Sir Wilfrid Laurier when he came to town. In their book *Edmonton—Portrait of a City*, Person and Routledge tell us that the King Edward was the first hotel in Edmonton to introduce bed-sitting room furniture designed specifically for hotel use.

You may be interested to know that the first taxi service in Edmonton was based at the King Edward Hotel. That happened back in the spring of 1913 when a gentleman named Robert M. Tryon from Calgary brought in a fleet of specially designed Fords. As suited the classy King Edward, these taxis were equipped with cigar lighters, flower vases, and meters. The drivers wore uniforms, and they and their cars fit right into the top-of-the-line hotel picture.

The King Edward was host hotel to some famous "firsts" in our city. In January 1912, a group of the city's more prominent ladies gathered and formed what became the Women's Canadian Club. There were some powerful names on the roster, including Mrs. Bulyea, the wife of the lieutenant-governor, Mrs. Sifton, and Mrs. Rutherford, wife of A. C. Rutherford. Mr.

The story of a city is often told through its hotels. In Edmonton, the King Edward Hotel has contributed more than its share of chapters to the Edmonton story.

Rutherford had served on the legislative assembly of the North-West Territories in 1902, moved on to the role of deputy speaker until 1905, and then became the first premier of the newly created Province of Alberta. Also part of the group was Mrs. McQueen, wife of Reverend Dr. McQueen of the First Presbyterian Church, and of course there was a lady called Emily Murphy. Emily Murphy led Alberta's Famous Five who, in 1929, won their fight to have women declared "persons" who could not only vote in elections but also sit in the Senate.

Emily Murphy was the first president of the Women's Canadian Club, and there is a marvellous photograph taken of the executive at their inaugural meeting where Emily is front and centre, as befits her position with the organization. The photograph was taken in the King Edward Hotel. The ladies are wearing immense hats, the style of the day, and there is an unfounded rumour that because the portion of the hotel where the photograph was taken was unfinished at the time, Emily Murphy is sitting on a wooden box. She looks very poised, though, and wooden box or chair, she is in command of the moment.

The hotel continued to serve Edmonton well over the years. Then, on April 24, 1978, a disastrous fire gutted the building. The shell sat behind wooden boards for almost a year before the decision was made to level rather than restore it.

And so the gracious old King Edward Hotel came down, and Manulife Place filled the site. Surely, though, the ghosts of the guests of the King Edward Hotel, and the building itself, are still there somewhere. Now if we could just see them and listen to their stories.

The Day the Movies
Came to Town

It was on a Tuesday night, July 28, 1908, when the movies came to Edmonton. Tuesday is a strange night, somehow. You might have expected it to be on a Friday or Saturday. But whether the night was right or not, the name of the theatre was certainly appropriate. It was called the Bijou, and there has to be a Bijou Theatre in everybody's life at one point or another.

You can get all tangled up in the name Bijou here in Edmonton. In the 1910 Henderson's Directory, there were two Bijou theatres listed, one on the north side and the other in Strathcona. It's the north side house that we're dealing with here, but you have to be careful. There is a photograph in the collection at the City of Edmonton Archives that shows the interior of the Bijou Theatre. From the looks of the rows of wooden kitchen chairs and the basic amenities, you might conclude that this was Edmonton's first movie house, but the photograph was actually taken in the Strathcona Bijou. It's safe to assume, though, that they both looked very much alike once you were inside.

A gentleman, and you might even go so far as to say a gentle man, called A. R. Lawrence opened the downtown Bijou in 1908, almost one hundred years ago now. Tony Cashman, the noted Edmonton historian, tells us that Mr. Lawrence arrived in town with the movie projector tucked into his luggage. There was some question, Tony tells us, as to whether the projector would have caused a problem coming through Canada Customs, but since nobody noticed it, it arrived here in town without questions being raised.

It's fascinating to find, again in the City of Edmonton Archives, a report in the *Edmonton Journal* that's dated November 20, 1958. This article gives us a picture and an interview with Mr. A. R. "Pop" Lawrence just before his ninetieth birthday. In the newspaper account, he talks of the day the pictures came to Edmonton.

Mr. Lawrence had come here to be a printer on the staff of the *Edmonton Journal*, but instead got into the movie business and was the narrator at the old Bijou. He talks of the poster that was displayed outside the theatre, which read "Last day to see *The Perils Of Pauline*," and Pop Lawrence reminisces about the line-up of kids waiting to see the twenty-minute film. Admission for a child was five cents, and while the theatre officially seated 240, they were able to squeeze in a few more of the little people. Just what the fire marshal would have to say about this today is another question, and there is no mention of a popcorn machine inside the Bijou. Apart from that, not much has changed over the years.

There was live theatre in Edmonton at the time, so there was some question as to whether the new form of entertainment would catch on and become a success. Well, that's another question that has been answered with the passage of time.

Once Pauline began to get into her perils on the screen at the front of the theatre, Pop Lawrence took up his position at the back of the theatre and in a loud, clear voice, narrated the story of what was appearing on the screen. Today I guess we would call it a "voice over," but we don't know what they called it in 1908.

The location of the downtown Bijou was on the west side of 100 Street

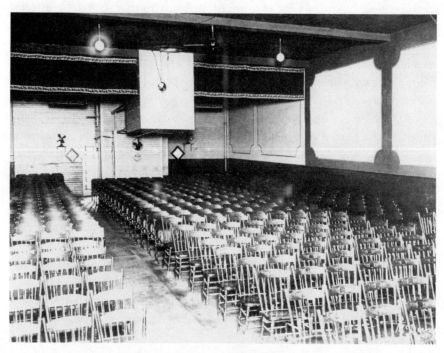

It was a little short on popcorn and soft drinks, but the Bijou
Theatre had everything else it needed to bring cinema to the city.

just south of 101A Avenue. That's roughly diagonally across the street from the Westin Hotel today.

At one time, the Edmonton post office was right next door to the Bijou, and it caught fire on October 17, 1907. Luckily the Bijou wasn't damaged, but the post office was destroyed. They rebuilt it on the opposite corner, where the Westin now sits. That's why today the old post office clock sits in its case in front of the hotel.

Things shuffled around a lot in the movie house business. There was more live theatre, more motion picture outlets, and more name chains. The old original Bijou moved to 101 Street where in time it became the Rialto Theatre. Back on 100 Street, the Bijou building stayed intact, but it, in turn, became a butcher shop. When the butcher shop first opened it was called Cheap John's Meat Market. Just how long it held onto that name we're not sure, but it became another meat market with the passage of time. On a cold January day in 1952 they were doing some remodelling at the Queen City Meat Market, at 10166 100 Street, when they found, under-neath the Queen City sign, evidence of the old Bijou Theatre—they were in the same location.

And that's how it all began, with Pop Lawrence at the back of the Bijou, giving the kids a play-by-play commentary on the *Perils of Pauline*.

They Dared to Call
Them Laddies

The Edmonton fire department did an interesting thing in 1908: it sold a little advertising, hired a graphic artist, took some photographs, and produced a booklet that told the story of the Edmonton fire department. It must have made interesting reading back then, and it certainly makes interesting reading today, some ninety-plus years later.

On the cover of the booklet is a drawing that shows the fire department responding to a call. The firemen are getting to the scene of the fire as quickly as they can, which means letting their horses gallop down the street. They're making good time at it, too, by the looks of the picture.

Then you open the front cover, and begin to read the story. The opening paragraphs tell the history of the original Edmonton fire brigade; they headline this portion, "OUR FIRE LADDIES."

As we read the first page we learn that the fire brigade gives 1892 as the date it came into being. That's when Edmonton became a town in its own right, and that's when the first volunteer corps was organized. The volunteer system continued until April of 1906, when:

> The paid system under the present popular and competent head of the department was organized and brought to its present state of perfection under his superintendence. Chief R. G. Davidson is regarded as one of the most efficient men in the employ of the city and the citizens have the utmost faith in his ability.

Excessive humility doesn't seem to have been a big concern, and they certainly knew how to say nice things about the boss.

In the second paragraph, the writers pay tribute to Tommy Lauder:

> The pioneer member of Edmonton's fire brigade, both volunteer and paid, is Tommy Lauder, now captain of the No. 1 station. Tommy Lauder was with the brigade at its inauguration and with the exception of one year he has been identified with it ever since.

You have to remember that this booklet was prepared in 1908. The writing style is enthusiastic, and it certainly brings a breath of fresh air to what sometimes takes the form of rather stodgy historical recording. Listen as they discuss the formation of the volunteer fire brigade.

It was on a bright mid-summer evening in June, sixteen years ago that the citizens of the town of Edmonton met at the office of P. Daly, who was then carrying on a drug business in the present Royal Shoe Store, Jasper Avenue east, "for the purpose of electing officers to manage and conduct the chemical engine, hook and ladder and general apparatus" which had just been purchased by the town council for the purpose of fire protection. Up to this time the town was at the mercy of the water bucket and the individual efforts of the residents.

You almost feel as though you were there, and from the quotation marks in their story, we can conclude that they even appointed a recording secretary.

And what did they have in the way of fire-fighting equipment? The first apparatus consisted of a village manual ladder truck and a manual double forty-gallon cylinder chemical unit. This equipment was stored in a shed at the rear of the new block erected by the Blowey-Henry Co. on Jasper Avenue. And it was "To this rendezvous all the citizens flocked when the call of the fire rang out in the early days of the city."

The shed they're talking about would have been about halfway between the Hotel Macdonald and the convention centre in today's terms, and right on the top of the riverbank.

Then the booklet goes on to tell us about what happened next:

In 1893 the present hall at the corner of Fraser Avenue and Rice Street [98 Street and 101A Avenue] was built and in the fall of that year the apparatus was moved to that building. In October a steam engine and two hand hose reels were purchased. In the new building was sleeping accommodation for twelve men with light, heat and water supplied free. The fees paid the brigade were at the rate of 60 cents an hour while in attendance at fires.

There may have been happy firemen, but there wouldn't have been any rich ones. Remember, too, that Edmonton didn't even have a water distribution system at the time. To fight the fires, the water for the steam engine came from tanks buried in the ground at strategic locations around town. There were eleven of these tanks, each of which held twelve thousand gallons of water, and it was the job of the steam engineer with the fire brigade to make sure that they were kept full.

The first chief under the new "paid" system was R. G. Davidson, who was brought in from Sherbrooke, Quebec, for the job. He arrived here on April 15, 1906.

In the spring of 1907 the installation of the Gamewell fire alarm system began. The first fire alarm called in over the new system was rung in on August 23, 1907. The installation of the system was carried out by members of the fire department under the direction of the department electrician, R. W. Border.

The booklet details the growth of the department and the addition of new fire stations. There are lots of pictures of the new halls and the horses that pulled the equipment. In some of the pictures, you can see the harnesses hanging from the ceiling of the fire hall, ready to be lowered onto the horses' backs when the fire alarm began to ring.

That's the way our fire department looked back in 1908, and a proud service it was, too.

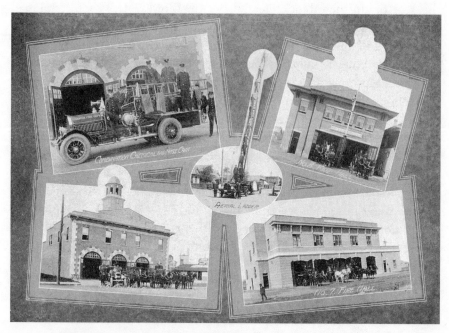

As Edmonton grew, so did Edmontonians' taste for fine fire halls, which were staffed with the bravest of men and state-of-the-art equipment.

Our Sound
of Music

The year was 1908, and Edmonton was a very different city than the one we know today. Street cars began operating on city streets that fall, the University of Alberta held its first classes in Strathcona, and our first motion picture theatre, the Bijou, opened on 100 Street at about 102 Avenue.

But surely the most interesting and important thing that happened that year was the sound of music that was heard in the city to a degree that it had never reached before. Edmonton had a music festival, the first held in Alberta and the first in Canada. Two men in particular, Vernon Barford and Howard Stutchbury, made it happen. They had a lot of help from their friends, but without those two it is doubtful that the concept would ever have become a reality.

In the beginning, it was never intended to be an Alberta thing at all. Governor General Earl Grey announced in 1907 that he would hold a competition open to all musical and theatrical talent in the country. We had a newly appointed lieutenant-governor here in Alberta, G. H. V. Bulyea, who was very anxious to show the rest of the country just what Alberta could do in such a competition. Between Edmonton and Strathcona, we had a total population of twenty-three very active theatrical and musical groups.

Lieutenant-Governor Bulyea got hold of Howard Stutchbury, one of the local leaders in the theatrical world. Stutchbury, in turn, brought Vernon Barford into the conversation because Barford was the central musical figure in town. While the two men were anxious to put together an entry into the competition, if it came to pass, and though there was no doubt that the talent was here, the cold financial facts were that we just couldn't afford to send a team to central Canada to compete.

But the idea was still a good one, whether the money was there to send an entry to Ottawa or not. Barford and Stutchbury kept the idea alive in their own minds and began to work on developing it. They talked to Bulyea, who was supportive, as were the local musicians when they were approached by Stutchbury and Barford. Out of all this came the first music

Vernon Barford made his way from Oxford University in England to All Saints Cathedral in Edmonton and stayed here for sixty-three years, leaving us a musical legacy that will never be equalled.

festival in Alberta, and, in fact, in Canada. It opened in May of 1908 in the All Saints' Cathedral in downtown Edmonton.

This was no small-scale festival, either. This was 1908, remember, but there were choirs, mixed choirs, quartets, soloists, and pianists. We brought in judges from Winnipeg: Rhys Eaton and James W. Matthews. The competitions were held in both McDougall Methodist Church and All Saints' Cathedral. The big windup was a concert held in the Thistle Rink that saw two thousand people come to hear the music. That first concert featured a two-hundred-voice chorus, a massed male chorus of one hundred voices, and a forty-piece orchestra.

They never looked back after that first festival. It became an annual event, and continued to grow. For the most part the only centre that held a bigger music festival over the years was Toronto, which had a few more people to draw upon for contestants.

But who were the two movers and shakers that got this started and kept it going? Vernon Barford was a unique character who came to Edmonton in 1900 after training in England with the choir at Worcester Cathedral and later at Oxford. He came to Edmonton to fill the role of organist and choirmaster at All Saints' Cathedral, which he held for fifty-six years. He did a lot of other things for the musical enlightenment of Edmonton over time as well, such as organizing the Edmonton Amateur Operatic Society in 1903. When Alberta became a province, it was Barford who conducted the orchestra and chorus in a massive gala at the Thistle Rink, and half a century later he held the same role when we celebrated our fiftieth anniversary as a province.

Stutchbury was also born in England, educated in eastern Canada, and had arrived in Edmonton in 1903. He worked well with Barford, and the two of them worked well with other members of the committee.

But there is a story behind the story of that first festival that shows what Edmonton was all about in 1908, quite apart from the cultural benefits of having people like Vernon Barford and Howard Stutchbury on the scene.

There was a young lady called Eva Blasdell. Eva had worked very hard to prepare herself for her appearance at that first music festival and arrived at All Saints' a little ahead of her scheduled performance time. Eva was fourteen years old then and had been a keen piano student since she was four. This was a major event in her musical life, perhaps the steppingstone to bigger and better things. Just as they were about to go into the church for her performance, Eva's mother realized that they had forgotten to bring the ticket Eva needed to make her appearance. So Eva's mom told her to wait, then went out into the street and flagged down a horse-drawn milk wagon. When Mrs. Blasdell told the driver about her predicament he drove her to the house on Ottawa Street (93 Street today) and back again in time for Eva's performance before the adjudicator. Eva went on to great accomplishments as a pianist, but ended up back in Edmonton when she married a young pilot called Harold Brooker. Did Eva ever regret marrying and settling down in Edmonton? Not according to her son, Bev Brooker.

Only in Edmonton, you say? Probably only in Edmonton could you have the first musical festival in the country and a career saved by a milkman.

This is quite a city.

The World's Shortest Railway

It must have seemed like a good idea at the time to build a railroad that was exactly two hundred feet long from beginning to end, but it lasted only four years before it was demolished. It was called the Edmonton Incline Railway, and the story behind it is intriguing.

There are a great many names linked with the early history of Edmonton, including Alex Taylor, Donald Ross, Matt McCauley, John Walter, and scores of others, both male and female. But ask someone what he or she remembers of old Joe Hostyn, and you are likely to draw a blank stare. Joseph Hostyn … hmmm. But he was the mover and shaker behind the idea of the inclined railway, and he made it a reality on May 20, 1908.

Joe wasn't alone in this venture, and had some fairly heavy financial guns backing him up. Among the directors of his company were such prominent Edmontonians as Donald Ross, Richard Secord, F. B. Hobson, Pete Anderson, and G. P. Blythe. Donald Ross was, of course, the owner and operator of the Edmonton Hotel, Richard Secord was one of our more successful businessmen, and while you may not recognize the name right away, Pete Anderson ran a very successful brickyard over where the Muttart Pyramids are today.

But who in the world was Joseph Hostyn? Joe Hostyn was the manager of Donald Ross's Edmonton Hotel. Now we know that there was a great deal of thinking and planning that took place in Donald's hotel, and presumably this scheme was part of it. Joseph Hostyn had seen the teams of horses working their way up the steep grade to the top of the riverbank, then making their way carefully back down again. It was hard work for the horses and it took ten to fifteen minutes to make the trip, even when the road was dry and safe. Why, Joe seems to have said, don't we build a hoist that will take teams, and pedestrians if they don't like the long climb, from the bottom of the hill to the top? Why don't we build it right outside the hotel? That way it will end up at the point where 101 Street meets the top of the bank.

It seems that a number of people thought the idea was good enough to

*It seemed like a good idea at the time, and when finished, the
Inclined Railway was Edmonton's shortest railway. It was
right in the heart of town, and has quite a story to tell.*

back it financially. The cost was estimated to be $16,000, but sadly for Joe and the board of directors, the final costs came in at just over the $30,000 mark.

At first, the thought was to power the hoist with electricity. Then the city took a long hard look at the amount of power it would take to drive the hoist motor and said that supplying electricity for the railway was out. So they converted to a one-hundred-horsepower steam engine.

Then they struck a fee structure. The cost was fifteen cents for a wagon and team, round trip, or ten cents one way, while foot passengers paid five cents. The hours of operation were from 7:00 AM to 7:00 PM. If there was something special going on down on the flats, such as a baseball game, and it looked as though there might be a little evening business, the railway stayed open.

There were all kinds of safety features built into the design, even to the point of a barrier that stopped frightened horses from backing off the platform if they became startled during the trip, which took about a minute.

Somebody once described it as being halfway between an outdoor escalator and a San Francisco cable car. There were two sets of tracks, each about twice as wide as a normal railroad track, and on them ran two cars that were linked together with a cable and pulley system that worked a little like a counterbalance. As one car went down, its weight helped pull the other car up, and if more power was needed, the steam engine provided it.

The wagons, teams, and foot passengers rode on moving platforms that were twenty feet wide and forty feet long. They could handle a reasonable load of freight, but the project was in trouble right from the start. They would keep the railway open after a baseball game down at the park in Rossdale, but there were a great many ball fans who would rather save the nickel and climb the wooden steps that paralleled the railway.

Teamsters, too, tended to take the old way up the hill when the weather was good, although they were quick enough to take advantage of the line when the hill was wet or icy. But it just wasn't a money-maker, because to reach the lower platform you had to drive your team partway up the hill anyway, so many teamsters thought it was just as easy to go all the way and save the money.

But what really brought it to its knees was the completion of the High Level Bridge in 1913. The owners were left with an inclined railway that nobody wanted. They could use the High Level for nothing, so why pay the fare on Hostyn's Hoist? Late in 1913 the hoist was shut down for good. Parts of it were broken up and hauled away, other bits of footings and things were left buried in the bank. It probably seemed like a good idea at the time, but ...

The North Saskatchewan River valley makes Edmonton unique and adds to the beauty of the city during all four seasons. It has to be admitted, though, that getting across the river and getting up the bank on the other side has been a transportation problem over the years.

One of the many answers to the climb-up-the-bank problem was our Inclined Railway. Unfortunately it was one of the shorter-lived answers.

Only in
Strathcona

Here is a marvellous story about an Edmonton clock. Recognizing the fact that those Edmontonians who live on the south side of the river are a little different, when you hear the story of this clock you can just about hear some north side individual saying, "Only in Strathcona!"

The clock in question is to be found in the south side post office building, on Whyte Avenue at 105 Street. The building stopped serving as a post office in November 1976. The windows were boarded up, the lights turned off, and the structure sat empty for almost ten years. But the south side post office had a clock in its tower, and the people of Strathcona were so used to looking up at the post office clock and checking the time that they were lost when the clock stopped.

They were so upset by this that they raised a clamour that was actually heard by the Federal Government in Ottawa. And, believe it or not, the government hired a man to come in to wind the clock and service it for the whole ten-year period that the building was closed. Only in Strathcona, do I hear you say?

The building itself has been around for a long time. It was originally called the Strathcona Public Building. There had been a smaller post office in Strathcona, but the need for a larger and more impressive federal presence was felt to be advisable. The planning and design process began in May 1908. The Federal Government purchased land from Dr. S. Archibald a year later, and construction began in 1910. The department of public works prepared the plans, under the direction of David Ewart, the chief Dominion architect.

There is a rather sad note connected with the Strathcona Public Building. Strathcona was incorporated as a town in 1899 and as a city in 1907. Like so many other western towns, it just sort of "growed" with a mixture of architectural types going up along the main street. But in the decade before the turn of the century and the decade after, there was a surge in the construction of more permanent structures, and the Strathcona Public Building was one of them. The sad note is that by the time the Strathcona

You might be surprised to find how important the clock in the south side Post Office tower was to the people who had grown accustomed to its face.

Public Building was completed and ready for occupancy in 1913, Strathcona had amalgamated with Edmonton the year prior, so technically there was no Strathcona any more.

The last part of the building to be completed was the part that the people of Strathcona feel so strongly about—the clock. It was built by J. Smith & Son, Midland Clockmakers, from Derby, England. On January 23, 1913, the *Edmonton Bulletin* proudly announced:

The new post office clock is on its way here. It has been shipped some days ago, and on its arrival will be installed in the tower by W. M. Reynolds, jeweller, of Whyte Avenue. The dial of the clock will be about four feet six inches in diameter. The bell weighs about 590 pounds and the whole apparatus will weigh about three tons.

The trouble started when the clock arrived: they found that it would not fit the space provided for it. The contractor said that the tower needed to be twelve feet higher. The architect felt that a cupola built on the roof would do the trick. But then it was decided that there wasn't room in the tower for the bell, and that the weights needed another ten feet of travel. The end result? They built a taller tower.

Then came 1952. The clock wasn't working, and what do you do with a three-ton clock? That year they called Bob Lang, and he came and fixed it.

And that's where the rest of this fascinating story kicks in. Bob Lang was really a locksmith, trained by Joel Lipsett right here in Edmonton. Bob had just bought his mentor's business, Joel's Locksmith, and as he points out, when you first go into business you don't say no to any job that's offered. When called he said that of course he could fix a clock at the post office. He thought they meant the timing device on a vault, but when he arrived and asked where he might find the clock that needed repair, people kept pointing up. And then he found out which clock they were talking about.

The repair turned out to be a mechanical one. Bob attended to it and has been looking after the clock ever since. He's the one who went in and wound it once a week when the building was closed. He's the one who serviced it twice a year, and he's also the one who moved the works down to the level of the second storey when the building was refurbished and put back into use.

Today you can sit beside the works of the post office clock and watch it tick away as you sip the refreshment of your choice and watch a game of billiards. The works, you see, are now part of the decor of the Billiard Club. You go in the east door of the old post office and up to the second floor, and there you are.

The works are the original equipment that came from England in 1913. They were installed in the tower but are now mounted on a solid base on one side of the Billiard Club. The movement is transmitted vertically with the aid of a metal rod that runs the hands on the clock face through what amounts to a differential gear, as you would find on an automobile. You can sit and watch the pendulum swinging back and forth. You can listen to the ticking as the mechanism does its thing, but you can't really listen to the bell chime.

The bronze bell is mounted in the overhead tower. You can look up and see it. But the chain and cable that actuate it are disconnected. It was pointed out by the patrons of the Billiard Club that when they were lining up a three-cushion bank shot the bonging of a six-hundred-pound bronze bell just over their heads tended to break their concentration.

A Skill-testing Question

This week's skill-testing question? Name the first building to be erected, occupied, and put to use on the campus of the University of Alberta. Actually, that's a bit of a trick question. The first building erected, occupied, and put into use on the campus had nothing to do with the University of Alberta at the time.

The building later became an integral part of the campus and is still in use today. You will perhaps recognize the name: it's called St. Stephen's College and you'll find it at 8820 112 Street, right in the heart of the campus.

When it first opened in 1911 it was known as Alberta College South. To tell the story of St. Stephen's you have to back up in time and tell the story of the beginning of Alberta College.

In 1903 the Edmonton District of the Methodist Church decided to proceed with the establishment of a college. The Reverend George McDougall, that early Edmonton clergyman, had willed a portion of his land to the church to be used for educational purposes. A group of interested people met on October 5, 1903, in a room above the old Johnstone Walker store, and by the time the meeting was over, they had a college. They didn't have a name, they didn't have a staff, they didn't have any buildings, they didn't have any students, but they did have a principal—Reverend J. H. Riddell. In time, the students came, and an association with McGill University was formed. The courses offered were guided from McGill by a man whose name would become famous in Alberta educational circles, Dr. Henry Marshall Tory. Dr. Tory moved west and became the first president of the University of Alberta.

They soon came up with a name for the college, too. They decided to call it Alberta College, a very fitting title. The minutes of a meeting of the board in 1908 outlined where the college was going to go next.

The establishment of the Provincial University in the city of Strathcona will mark a new era in the progress of higher education in

113

St. Stephen's College was the first building on the University of Alberta Campus, but in the beginning it didn't have anything to do with the university. This interesting building can still be seen on campus today.

Alberta. It is the purpose of the Board to seek the closest possible affiliation with the University and to cooperate in every way with the Government to build up a thorough educational system in the province.

Within a few months, the principal, Dr. Riddell, was in the middle of the trees on the south bank of the North Saskatchewan, supervising the clearing of the site that would be the location of Alberta College South. It's significant to note that the location of the University of Alberta was by no means settled at this time. There was a strong lobby from Calgary demanding that it be built in the south. The sod-turning ceremony for the Arts Building on the Edmonton campus didn't take place until September 29, 1909, lending some strong support to the contention that the creation of Alberta College South was a major factor in the decision to make Edmonton the site of the university.

While all this was going on, Dr. McQueen of First Presbyterian Church, along with Dr. John MacEachran, a philosophy professor at the university, persuaded the general assembly of the Presbyterian Church that Edmonton needed a theological college. This led to the opening of Robertson College, which was located in two houses on 76 Avenue and 106 Street. This, in turn, led to the construction of a brick building to house Robertson College on Whyte Avenue and 110 Street. The Methodists, on the other hand, were offering theological training at Alberta College South. Shortly after the Presbyterians and the Methodists got together to found the United Church in 1925, it was decided to combine the two theological programs in one location—Alberta College South. And that's when the name was changed to St. Stephen's College.

Dr. George Tuttle was principal of St. Stephen's from 1966 to 1979, and we are indebted to him for some interesting historical notes on the college:

> Over the years, the building was used in more ways than one can easily remember. For the first decade, young men and women in the matriculation department occupied some floors. They studied math and English just down the hall from a more senior group of men developing their speciality in theology. Both were inevitably aware of a flourishing music department, which later was transferred back to Alberta College North.
>
> From 1917 to 1920 the facilities were on loan to the government as a convalescent hospital for veterans.

And that's when one of the aspects of the building, an aspect remembered by so many University of Alberta students, was added. Two green cylindrical steel columns were added to the exterior. These were specially designed fire escapes for the patients, who, in an emergency, would have been popped into the fire escape and then spiralled down to ground level and safety.

In World War II the north wing housed No. 2 Army Training Corps. In the thirties and forties, the University Hospital took over the south wing as a nurses' residence.

And today? Well, St. Stephen's College is a designated resource building, has been partially restored, and is occupied, fittingly enough, by Alberta Culture's Historic Resources Division.

The upper floors are still untouched since their early days, and you can walk the musty corridors in the company of peeling paint, dusty woodwork, and the odd bat, along with a host of ghosts and memories.

Not Just
Any School

A school is more than a school when it's a major part of Edmonton's scholastic history, even though most of the people of the city don't realize it.

Sitting quietly on the south side of 78 Avenue between 106 and 107 Streets is a stately, old, red-brick schoolhouse that's been around since 1906. It is the second-oldest operating school in Edmonton, but that's only one of its claims to fame. It also happens to be the building in which the first classes of the University of Alberta were held, but let's get back to the beginning of the story.

Today the building is called Queen Alexandra School, but even the name has changed since the school first opened its doors to students. One of the early mayors of Strathcona was a gentleman called S. S. Duggan. To honour the gentleman, they named a street after him. Duggan Street became 78 Avenue when the numbering system came to town. When they built this school and opened it for students on February 5, 1906, they did the only sensible thing—they named it the Duggan Street School. Life was simpler in 1906.

Then came October 7, 1910, and someone in their wisdom decided that the school needed a more formal name. They chose Queen Alexandra, in honour of the consort of King Edward VII. The queen was so pleased that she sent an autographed picture of herself to the school, a picture that is still an honoured part of the school memorabilia.

But before the name of the school was changed from Duggan Street to Queen Alexandra, it managed to pick up another claim to fame. The University of Alberta had come into being and was to be based in Edmonton. All of which was fine, but the students at the new university had nowhere to go to hold their classes. That's where the Duggan Street School came into the picture. Dr. Henry Marshall Tory, the first president of the university, opened an office in the Duggan Street School. The first forty-five students at the newly created university met for their classes in the school's assembly room on the third floor.

An interesting historical side story to all this has to do with the door to Dr. Tory's office. It had painted on it, "Office of the President." It's not every school that has a university president's office in its building, so this was a real honour. Later, in the 1950s, the school underwent some major renovations. In the course of a visit to Queen Alexandra to see how the work was progressing, then-superintendent W. P. Wagner noticed a glazed door on its way to the rubbish heap and realized what it was. It was the door with that simple message painted on the glass: "Office of the President." Wagner rescued the door and carefully packed it away for safekeeping. On the occasion of the fiftieth anniversary of the University of Alberta in 1958, the Edmonton Public School Board presented the door to the university as a gift. The school itself was actually built in two parts. The first half, the eastern portion, was completed in 1906. The western portion was built in 1913 to meet the need for an increased number of students.

When the first section was opened in 1906, the *Strathcona Plain Dealer* reported:

The six-room building is of very handsome design. It is fitted with all modern conveniences, including electric lights, steam heat, water and sewerage, and the most approved systems of ventilation and fire protection.

That may have been true about the fire protection, but they didn't add fire escapes until 1909, and at the same time they cleared some trees from the property so that a telephone line could be run in.

And what was it like to be a student at the Duggan Street School in 1909? Well, if you were in grade one you practised your lessons using a piece of slate and some chalk. That did you until you reached grade four. In grade four you were introduced to a lead pencil and a notebook. That did you for another two grades, and finally in grade six you learned how to use a pen and ink.

There are some interesting pieces of Edmonton memorabilia built into the Queen Alex story. One of the teachers was Mr. Harry Ainlay. One of Mr. Ainlay's students was a young man called Dudley Menzies. The two worked together years later, when Harry Ainlay was mayor of Edmonton and young Dudley Menzies was a city commissioner.

And in an age when audio-visual equipment is a standard part of the sophisticated teaching equipment at any school, former Principal Murray MacDonald tells of the time after he became principal in 1942 when it was decided that the school day would begin with a recitation of the Lord's Prayer. There was a record player near his office, and he happened to own a recording of John Charles Thomas singing the Lord's Prayer. So every morning at 9:00 the teachers would open their classroom doors and MacDonald would put the record on the gramophone and play the Lord's Prayer. It worked like a charm, to the point where one young man in grade one remarked to his teacher that Mr. MacDonald had a pretty good singing voice for a school principal.

That's the way things were at the good old Queen Alex, another interesting piece in Edmonton's history.

The Queen Alexandra School is the only school in the province that remembers when the University of Alberta could be found established in its top-floor gymnasium.

"Peace River"
Jim Cornwall

Every once in a while you come across a character who is larger than life, and it's always a thrill to find that they lived right here in Edmonton.

There is a beautiful house overlooking Groat Ravine just south of 102 Avenue. It was built in 1912 and was the home of Mr. James Cornwall and his family. Unless you dig a little deeper, you would never realize just what a colourful character Mr. Cornwall turned out to be.

He was born in Brantford, Ontario, in 1869, and before he died in Calgary in 1945 at the age of seventy-six, he had made and lost two fortunes, and built his gracious home in Edmonton. He did a few other things along the way, and that's where the story of "Peace River" Jim takes on a life of its own.

The story starts in Brantford, but it doesn't stay there for very long. Jim Cornwall left home at the age of fifteen and sold newspapers on the streets of Buffalo, New York, before he got a job on a sailing ship working the Great Lakes. He moved from the Great Lakes ship to salt water sailing, and worked his way around the world three times on a windjammer.

He was a trader, but his luck ran out playing the Chicago Grain Exchange, and he lost everything. He made his way west, got a job building the railroad through the Crowsnest Pass, and when that job finished, came to our part of the world and set himself up as a fur trader. His first trading post was at Grouard, but before long he had established a string of fur trading posts that stretched from Edmonton to Inuvik.

The Cornwall home on Groat Ravine covered some ten thousand square feet, and one of the features was a large library. Jim Cornwall never did finish the floor in that room, because that's the room in which he traded furs with the Indians, and since the floor was always covered with furs anyway, why put down good hardwood?

Cornwall was always a strong spokesman for the benefits and potential of the Peace River country. That's where he got the nickname of Peace River Jim. He didn't seem to be able to talk about anything else at the time.

After he made Edmonton his base in 1897, he began to talk up the need

119

for mail service to the Peace River area. Somebody in the equivalent of Canada Post at the time suggested that if he felt the Peace River country should have mail service, he'd have to deliver it himself. So he did. On foot.

It was a twenty-one-day trip when the trail was good, and thirty days when it wasn't. But Jim got mail service started to the Peace River country, and it has never stopped.

Settled in his house, The Villa, after it was completed in 1912, he kept up his interest and activities in the north. In 1915 he discovered oil at the deposit that became known as the Norman Wells field.

By this time, World War I was in full swing, and Cornwall organized and led the 218th Battalion Irish Guards. It sounds like a formidable fighting force, but in fact it was a construction battalion that made a real contribution to the war effort. Cornwall was colonel of the regiment, and was recognized with a Distinguished Service Order in 1918.

He operated the first paddle steamers on northern Alberta rivers, and he was on the first flight over the northern Polar Sea. This business of airplane flights over the north country he knew so well intrigued him. He organized the first regular air service to that part of the world, basing the operation at Edmonton as the southern terminus.

His grasp of the ways of the north and its peoples was something he earned, and earned the hard way. He spoke Cree, Slavey, Chipewyan, Dogrib, and three Inuit dialects.

This larger-than-life character had a tender side, too. He was a friend of another legend, Twelve Foot Davis. When Davis died in 1900, he was buried in a conventional grave. But Jim Cornwall and Davis had talked about where they would like to be buried, and Cornwall knew that Davis didn't have an ordinary cemetery in mind.

It was Peace River Jim Cornwall who had Davis's body exhumed, and moved to the special spot on the top of the riverbank overlooking the Peace River and its valley that they had both grown to know and love.

And that's where Twelve Foot Davis rests today, just sort of keeping an eye on things for himself and his old friend and partner, Peace River Jim Cornwall. And we sometimes think that Edmonton doesn't have any colourful characters in its history. Ha!

A Year to Remember

For pure, unadulterated excitement, the year 1912 was probably the biggest and best we've ever had. The year before, 1911, there were 24,900 of us living on the north side of the river in Edmonton, with another 5,579 in Strathcona. That's a total of 30,479. The figures for 1912 show a total population of about 50,000 souls, which means a 64% increase in one year. The 1912 figure is an approximation primarily because there were so many people pouring into town that they couldn't get them all to stand still long enough for an accurate count.

There are photographs at the City of Edmonton Archives that catch this city of ours in that memorable year, and you can spend a lot of time just looking at them and wondering how in the world they coped with it all.

There is one picture that looks as though it could be used to promote an old John Wayne cowboy movie. There is the little cattle town, the mud streets, the covered wagon with a team of oxen pulling it through the quagmire, and people standing at the edge of the road in period costumes. Except this isn't Dodge City in its heyday. This is Edmonton in 1912! And if the building in the background looks familiar, that's all right too. That building is still standing today: it's the YMCA building on 102A Avenue, and in the photograph, you're looking to the east from about 102 Street.

The year 1912 was when Strathcona and Edmonton amalgamated, and it was also the year that North Edmonton was annexed and became part of greater Edmonton. Building permits were up 400% over the previous year, and along the south side of Jasper Avenue there was a short stretch of businesses that housed no less than twenty-three separate real estate offices. There were thirty-two real estate brokers in town, 135 different financial agencies, and 336 registered real estate agents.

Proving once again that what goes up must come down, it's rather sad to note that by 1914, almost all of these people and their businesses had left the local scene. But in 1912 we were riding the wave, and one figure alone tells the real estate story. If you wanted to buy a piece of property along

Jasper Avenue in the business district it was going to cost you $10,000 a lineal foot. And that, remember, is in 1912 dollars.

Everywhere you looked major construction projects were underway: the Legislature Building was coming together, the High Level Bridge was nearing completion, we had opened the Dawson Bridge, and both the Tegler Building and the McLeod Building were close to completion.

The second photograph from the City Archives is taken the same year, but it shows a different section of the downtown area and is a strange mix of the familiar and the unfamiliar. You're looking to the north and east from 104 Street at about 100 Avenue. There is so much to see in the picture that you really need a guided tour to even *begin* to realize the Edmonton history present in that one photographic negative.

Gone but not forgotten is the Thistle Rink. You'll spot the domed roof of the Thistle just beyond the latticework appearance of the wooden forms in place for the new Hudson's Bay Building.

The Thistle was Richard Secord's pride and joy. He built it in 1902 on the east side of 102 Street just north of Jasper Avenue. It seated 1,500 people, and quite apart from the hockey and the curling that took place under its roof, it also was the home of the first sitting of the new Alberta Legislature when we became a province. They held it in the Thistle because

On those days when downtown traffic is heavy, parking stalls are full, and you don't have change for a meter, it helps to ponder the state of affairs in the good old days.

it was the biggest building in town, and it was big not just in Edmonton terms. It was the largest enclosed building anywhere on the prairies west of Winnipeg. It caught fire on Halloween in 1913, the year after this picture was taken, and was destroyed.

On the right-hand side of the picture you can spot the steel work of Kenny McLeod's contribution to the skyline, the McLeod Building. You can see the Tegler Building going up as well, and between the Tegler and McLeod buildings there is the old Civic Block. This is the building that started out as a six-storey warehouse, and ended up housing all the departments of the civic administration until the "new" city hall was completed and opened in 1957.

Tucked in there, too, are McDougall and Secord's Empire Block, and the Lyceum Theatre. And in the middle of the picture is a rather prominent church that doesn't look at all familiar. You might be surprised to find that this was the First Presbyterian Church, which, at the time, was located on the southwest corner of 103 Street and Jasper Avenue.

It was quite a year back in 1912, and when you think that within a couple of blocks of all that activity in the very centre of the city there was a covered wagon pulled by a team of oxen along a muddy street, well, all you can say is that this was Edmonton in 1912, and that about sums it up.

It Was the Biggest
Game in Town

It was May 13, 1912, and when we read about it today, it's hard to believe that it really happened. But it did happen, right here in Edmonton, and we are indebted to a former *Edmonton Journal* editor, A. Balmer Watt, for pulling the pieces together and putting it all down on paper.

The year was 1912. Edmonton was riding an economic wave that everyone felt would go on forever. Flickerings of economic distress were being felt in other parts of the world, but not in Edmonton. And one of the hottest commodities on the market here was real estate. Prices had escalated dramatically, and speculation was really running wild.

In the middle of all this, the Hudson's Bay Company, which held a large piece of land right in the middle of all the activity, was being pressured to put a major portion of its land up for sale. The Bay finally decided to cash in on the real estate boom, and so laid plans to put its property on the market. It made a modern-day rock concert look pale in comparison. At one point there were over two thousand people lined up for a chance to buy a piece of the action. But let's look at what led up to this massive queue that saw people sitting up all night for a chance to buy some building lots.

This following story ran in the *Edmonton Journal* in May of 1912:

With Edmonton in giddy excitement, the Hudson's Bay Reserve goes on the market. Today, on a first come, first served basis, 1,500 sale admission tickets are being distributed. Tomorrow, before sales begin, a lottery will be conducted. Tickets drawn in that lottery will determine the order in which choice of lots will be allocated. Each lottery ticket will entitle the holder to buy up to four lots.

The layout of the lots, along with price lists and descriptive literature were distributed. People saw this as a chance to make a fortune and the hysteria grew by the hour. With all the excitement, the Bay officials realized that there would be a stampede to line up for the draw tickets, so they kept the place of the "raffle" a secret, or so they thought.

A gentleman called F. T. Aitken was downtown and spotted a group of Hudson's Bay employees carrying a metal safe into the Gospel Mission Hall. The Gospel Mission was a small building on the east side of 103 Street about halfway between 102 and 103 Avenues. Aitken decided that this was where the draw was to be held, so he very quietly took up a position outside the door of the mission and began his long wait.

Aitken's guess was right on. And it wasn't long before a lot of other Edmontonians came to the same conclusion. Soon, the line-up behind Aitken was two thousand people long. Remember that this was just a line-up to get a ticket that entitled you to a place in the line-up to buy four building lots, and that the draw wasn't going to take place until the next day.

People camped out overnight. There were a few women sprinkled into the predominantly male line-up. It was a chilly night. There were people who wandered up and down the line selling coffee and sandwiches. Small boys flogged chairs. The price of a chair ranged from $1 to $5, depending on the condition and comfort level of the chair. Pillows cost $1, camp cots $25, and blankets brought prices that varied to extremes. Some men bought a blanket, curled up in it, and slept on the hard sidewalk.

The next morning dawned clear and bright. People offering ice cream and lemonade replaced the coffee vendors of the night before. As the day went on, it got hotter and hotter under the Alberta sun. Then along came the vendors offering cotton umbrellas, fetching $4 apiece. Straw hats were $5.

As the morning passed, the Bay personnel went down the line handing out numbered tickets confirming your place in line. This cut down on the possibility of people muscling their way into the line-up. Then the bartering for the numbered tickets began. The man up there at the door, F. T. Aitken, was offered $1,500 for his number. And all that number meant was that he would step inside the mission door and be given a chance to draw on what order he would line up to be allowed to buy four building lots.

At 2:00 PM the first twenty-five people in line were allowed into the mission, and the draw got underway. Police Chief Lancey was there to keep an eye on things, as well as Dr. McQueen, the Presbyterian clergyman. Aitken, the first one through the door, drew ticket #910. He would have his choice of lots after 909 other people made their pick. Finally, James Walsh, a retired farmer, drew ticket #1. He had first pick at the lots on sale, although he was the 928th person to pick.

Walsh had to leap over a fence and run back to his hotel after people learned of his good luck. The bidding for Walsh's ticket began at $20,000, and at last report was up to $27,000.

And what did Mr. Walsh buy? Two lots on 101 Street, priced at $25,000 each.

And shortly after things settled down, the bottom fell out of the real estate market and the subdivision offered by the Bay stood empty for many years. The paved street that was to bisect the area, called Portage Avenue, had streetcar tracks placed down the middle, but no streetcar ever used them. Portage Avenue became Kingsway after the king and queen visited here in 1939, and today we have forgotten almost everything about the biggest lottery in the city's history, the Hudson's Bay land sale, in May of 1912.

Seventy-seven Trombones

All well and good for Professor Harold Hill to sing about seventy-six trombones when he was selling the idea of a boys' band in River City. But when it comes to boys' bands, Edmonton isn't going to let River City steal the limelight. If it takes seventy-seven trombones to do it, just count 'em.

Edmonton had a boys' band back in 1913. The late John Michaels organized the *Edmonton Journal* Newsboys Band in 1913 as a means of reducing juvenile delinquency. That old Newsboys Band played for servicemen leaving Edmonton to fight in World War I, and the band made its first international appearance when it accompanied the Shriners to their 1916 convention in Buffalo, New York. Its finest hour came when the

The Edmonton Newsboys Band, seen here in 1924, started with someone's vision of keeping young boys off the streets and out of trouble. It became a musical success story, quickly winning international acclaim.

Prince of Wales invited the group to play at the 1924 British Imperial Exposition in Wembley, England.

And the band did just that: it travelled to England and played for the prince. Boys' bands from Edmonton do that sort of thing.

The Newsboys Band gradually faded from the local musical scene, but they were replaced in the fall of 1935 when a new organization appeared. It was called the Edmonton Schoolboys Band, under the direction of T. V. Newlove. There were forty-two players in that first band, but it didn't take long to grow.

The rules in 1935 were the rules that stayed with the band all the years that it played. A young man didn't even have to own an instrument to become a member. He just needed to want to play. The instrument and instruction were provided at a nominal cost if the student could afford them, and free if not.

Two years later the band had grown to sixty members, and Newlove took them all to Banff for a two-week vacation. It was a playing vacation, in that the band would parade up and down Banff Avenue to draw a crowd and then stage a small concert in the park adjacent to the Bow River. Newlove would address the crowd at some point, telling them how much the band boys ate, and then a collection would be taken to help offset the cost of the trip. The Banff trip proved to be such a successful climax to a year of rehearsing and playing that it was repeated in 1938, and again in 1939.

A high percentage of the band members were from what, today, we would refer to as inner city schools. McCauley School was the band's base. That's where Newlove was a full-time teacher, and many of the members were students at McCauley. They didn't think of themselves as being from an inner city school. They just came from families that didn't have a lot of disposable income.

Newlove would scrounge what he could in the way of free groceries, he would arrange for the band to march in the Calgary Stampede parade for a fee, and he would make a deal with the CPR and Edmonton Motors for rail and truck transportation from Edmonton to Banff. The band boys would go to Banff for two weeks, travelling by rail. The princely sum of $5 per member covered transportation, all the food they could eat, and accommodation in tents in Banff. And if your family didn't have the $5? Looking back on it now, one comes to the realization that Newlove always found the money somewhere. Nobody was left behind.

It was 1939 when majorettes were first introduced to the band, and there were majorettes on that 1939 Banff trip. Those mountain trips, and many of the other band functions, couldn't have taken place without Mrs. Jessie Newlove, who poured countless hours into support activities.

The band played at football games at Clarke Stadium, basketball games when the Edmonton Commercial Grads took on all comers at the Edmonton Gardens, and there were always the parades and the semi-annual concerts at the old Empire Theatre.

World War II hit the band hard. There were over 150 band members who signed up for active service, and there was a five-month period when the band shut down because their leader, T. V. Newlove, had joined the RCAF. He was discharged shortly after he enlisted, picked up his teaching load, and with the support of an assistant bandmaster, O. W. Murray, brought the band back to life and vigour.

Over the years, some thirteen hundred young Edmontonians, including fifty young ladies, were members of this unique Edmonton organization. The band went out of existence in 1969, but all those old horn blowers still gather and reminisce about the golden days of the Edmonton Schoolboys Band.

River City eventually got its boys' band, according to the musical that played at the Citadel Theatre, but no matter how good they became, they would never really be able to compete with Edmonton's Schoolboys Band.

Selling the Exhibition

When Klondike Days roll around each year, Edmonton is awash in raft races, fireworks, parades, and all kinds of fun things. They are designed to draw our attention to the fact that the Edmonton summer exhibition is with us again, and we are all encouraged to participate.

Each year the challenge is there for the organizers: how to make this summer festival interesting, vital, and worthy of the enthusiastic support of Edmontonians. Each year poses its own challenges, but one of the harder sells must have been in the summer of 1916. World War I was in full battle; things weren't going all that well for the Allies, and a great many of the local men were in the armed forces, many of them in Europe already, where news from the front was not good.

The Exhibition Association had used airplanes in previous years, and they tried it again in 1916. They called in a young lady from Texas. She came to Edmonton with her airplane, put on a dramatic show over the Exhibition Grounds, and tied the whole thing into the war effort.

Her name was Katherine Stinson, a full 105 pounds of classy lady, and she could make an airplane do amazing things. Katherine Stinson is the woman behind the story of the first delivery of airmail in western Canada. On July 10, 1918, Katherine flew up from Calgary in two hours and five minutes and turned a sack of mail over to the local postmaster.

That 1918 flight was her third visit to Edmonton, but in 1916 she was in town for the first time. She was twenty years old and a partner in a flying school in San Antonio, Texas. And during her stay here, she charmed the city.

The hoopla started in the newspapers in early July 1916. An advertisement in the *Edmonton Journal* said, "Sell your Hammer and Buy a Horn." Just what they meant by that isn't clear, but the advertisement went on to say that the Edmonton Exhibition was coming to town from July 10 to 15, and would feature "Finest Attractions, Best Exhibits ever seen in the province of Alberta, including KATHERINE STINSON, sensational Aviator."

*Katherine Stinson was, in every sense of the word, a lady. A legend
was born in 1918 when she delivered a sack of mail from Calgary
to Edmonton in her airplane, landing it safely at the fairgrounds.*

There were other attractions, true, high-class vaudeville artists, shows on the midway, military manoeuvres by "A" Squadron, 19th Alberta Dragoons, and a spectacular musical ride. But there was no doubt about it— Katherine Stinson was the big attraction.

She arrived with her 1913 Martin bi-plane and stayed at the Macdonald Hotel. She was photographed sitting on the edge of the cockpit of her plane, leather boots and all. When she was interviewed, she came up with some quotations that the newspaper was happy to use. We must remember that this was 1916, and flying was very new to Edmontonians. "Flying," said Miss Stinson, "is perfectly safe as long as you keep your head." She must have kept her head while she was demonstrating her skills over the crowds at the Exhibition Grounds, because her show was a roaring success.

The newspaper accounts report that she, along with her sister and brother, operated a flying school in San Antonio. Since the war started, they had trained sixty Canadian pilots, fifty-nine of whom had joined the Royal Flying Corps in England and were involved in the air war over France. One of their graduates was an Edmonton man, George Turnbull. Turnbull had travelled to Texas earlier that spring, completed his training, and was by then over in England. This was a short, snappy course. One of their graduates had finished the entire course in two weeks, when it normally took students six weeks to graduate.

"Canadian men make splendid fliers," said Miss Stinson in the course of her interview. "They are so strong, physically fit, and they have an object in view. They take their training seriously. They are different from the American men. With them flying is more of a fad and they take it lightly." How can you argue with that kind of public relations approach?

Edmonton was going through a turbulent time when Miss Stinson first came to town in 1916. Quite apart from the war effort, prohibition had reached Alberta, and legally we were a dry province. There was an outbreak of illegal drinking establishments and a general unhappiness about the way the whole thing was being handled.

The current news wasn't all black though. It's interesting to note that just the year before, a team of high school girls had won the provincial basketball championship, and had come back in 1916 to win it again. Their coach was a gentleman called J. Percy Page, and we can only guess that his young basketball team was there at the Exhibition Grounds watching Katherine Stinson perform her aerobatics for the crowd. It's likely that none of them, including their coach, ever dreamed that as the Edmonton Commercial Grads they would go down in sports history as the greatest basketball team ever assembled, or that their fame would rival that of the charming aviatrix who was flying above them at the Exhibition Grounds.

Katherine and her airplane came back to Edmonton the following year and again in 1918 on her airmail run. But she first came to town in 1916 to help with the promotion of the Edmonton Exhibition, and she did a marvellous job.

The Toonerville Trolley

If you want to be sticky about it, you are right. The original Toonerville Trolley was a streetcar line in a comic strip, but Edmonton had its own version of the Toonerville Trolley line, and it is fondly remembered by all those who used it.

This was a streetcar line that served the McKernan's Lake district for almost thirty-five years. There have been buses that have tried to take the place of the old streetcar, and they travel roughly the same route. But they will never be quite the same. To understand all of this, we have to pause for a minute and explain what McKernan's Lake is all about to those geographically disadvantaged Edmontonians who haven't heard where the name came from.

James McKernan was one of the original NWMP constables who made the trek to Fort Macleod in 1874. He took his discharge a couple of years later and went back to Ontario, but never quite got his memories of the west and this part of the world out of his mind. A couple of years after that, he and his brother Robert came back west to work on the telegraph line that stopped at Hay Lakes, close to Edmonton. Robert McKernan brought his family out from Ontario in 1878, and they set up house on the shore of a little lake a few miles south of the North Saskatchewan River. This little body of water became known as McKernan's Lake. It's drained now and covered with residential housing, but if you wanted to locate it geographically within the city, you would say that it was an area south of 76 Avenue and west of 111 Street. McKernan's Lake was close enough to town that it became a favourite recreational area for people who lived on both the north and south sides of the river.

In the 1912 boom period, McKernan's Lake became the place to go for sports, both in winter and summer. In winter, you could skate, curl, or take a trip on the toboggan slide that was built just south of the avenue.

And then the Edmonton streetcar system began to reach out with what they called stub lines, and one November Sunday in 1913, the streetcar service was extended far enough to reach the north shore of McKernan's

Lake. All of a sudden, access to this playground was cheap and handy. Within weeks there was a demand for electric lights to enhance the after-dark activities on the lake, and by New Year's Eve in 1913 there were enough lights, tents, and shacks already set up for the convenience of the skaters that a massive celebration was held, complete with fireworks and the whole ball of wax.

All the years that the streetcar line was in service, the track bed was always a little questionable. The streetcars would rock and roll along their route. They started at Whyte Avenue and 104 Street, ran south to 76 Avenue, then turned west and ran as far as 116 Street. At first there was a loop that had been built beside the lake, where the cars could turn around and head back down the track the way they had come. But with the passage of time the loop was taken out and one of the distinctive features of the Toonerville Trolley came into play. The cars had two trolleys, with controls at both ends. When the streetcar driver, or conductor as he was called, reached the end of the line, he would step outside the car, pull down on the rope attached to the end of the trolley and hook it to the roof of the car. He would then walk to the other end of the car and unhook the trolley at that end, raise it until it made contact with the overhead wire, and the car was ready to roll. Of course he also had to take the control levers from one end, walk to the other, and install them on the switch boxes there, but that took only a few seconds. He could also flip the backs of the seats from one side to the other so that the passengers were facing in the direction that the car was travelling, but quite often the passengers did that for him.

Not only that, but it almost served as a rural railway. People would stop the streetcar and hand the conductor a package or parcel that they wanted passed on to someone farther down the line. And he always took the parcel and delivered it to the recipient. There were people along the route whom the conductors knew were having difficulty getting out and about for some reason. So the conductors did what seemed reasonable—they dropped off the milk and the groceries that people couldn't get out to buy on their own. The Toonerville Trolley was like that. It was truly a neighbourhood streetcar line.

The Toonerville Trolley line carried on right through the years of the First and Second World Wars and all the years in between. The connections to other parts of Edmonton varied from time to time. All the streetcars were colour-coded so that Edmonton passengers knew where the cars were headed as they waited at the stops. The cars carried metal plates, front and rear, that displayed either a single colour or a combination of two. Red, white, and blue, with green on occasion. The red and green cars ran to Calder, the white to the Highlands, and so on. The McKernan Lake car carried a red and blue sign, and not everybody remembers that.

Right up to the mid 1940s, Edmontonians would often take the Toonerville Trolley to the end of the line during the winter months. They couldn't skate on McKernan's Lake any more, but they could ski at Whitemud, and there were a lot of happy snow skiers who rode the streetcar to and from a weekend afternoon on the snow. And they were never too tired to help flip the seats when it came time for the return trip to Whyte Avenue and 104 Street.

But all good things must come to an end, or so someone seemed to think. And it was a sad Saturday night in August of 1947 when the last Toonerville Trolley run ended at Whyte Avenue. They put on the buses, but they never quite erased the memory of the good old Toonerville Trolley.

This Is the House
that Jack Built

There is a princess living on the south side who celebrates her birthday on March 8 each year, because that's the date, in 1915, when she first opened. She's in remarkably good health for a lady that age, and her life story is a fascinating chapter in the history of this city.

The princess was the dream of a fellow called John Wellington (Jack) McKernan, and his life story, though short, is an interesting one in itself.

John McKernan was the nephew of James McKernan. James McKernan was one of the original members of the North West Mounted Police. Born in Ontario, James came west with the troops who made their historic trip in 1874. He had joined the police force the year before to see a bit of the world and have a taste of adventure. He got both in the course of that trip west, and he liked Edmonton and the surrounding area so much that he put down roots here. He was joined by his brother Robert in November of 1878, and John McKernan was the first child born to Robert and his wife, Sara. That was in the fall of 1880. The McKernan brothers farmed in an area of the south side that carries their name to this day. We know it as the McKernan Lake district, and if we were to check into it thoroughly we would find that the proper name is McKernan's Lake and that there were three, not one, bodies of water involved.

John McKernan was an entrepreneur. He was a financial success in that boom period in Edmonton's history leading up to World War I, and his dream was to build a theatre that would make an outstanding contribution to the Edmonton entertainment and cultural scene. The answer to that dream was the Princess Theatre. It began its turbulent history on March 8, 1915, ten months late, and came on stream at the wrong time. The idea was a good one, but the timing was all wrong.

The *Edmonton Bulletin* ran a feature story on the new theatre the day that it opened. The opening paragraph gives a good example of some journalistic standards as well:

When looking for the first time at the new Princess Theatre which opens upon its career of entertainment this afternoon at 2:00 p.m. on Whyte Avenue, one is struck by the faith in the growing power of the cinematograph to hold and influence public thought that has been the moving factor behind the building of this beautiful theatre and the extent to which the citizens of Edmonton have already shown an appreciation for the higher productions of the motion picture machine supports the conviction of the Princess Management that the new venture will be attended with success.

To use a line from a former editor of the *New Yorker* magazine, if you tapped that sentence on one end with your finger, it would go on rocking forever.

The front of the building was covered with marble, brought in from British Columbia. The rest of the materials came from Edmonton or the Edmonton area, which led to that same *Edmonton Bulletin* story being given the headline, "Made-In-Edmonton Theatre Opens Today On South Side."

There were two levels of seating, with a capacity of 660 patrons. It was the only building west of Winnipeg to have a marble front, and the lobby floor had marble tile. It had stained glass over the top of the double front doors, and the same high standards were to be found throughout the whole structure.

But the timing was bad. The bottom fell out of the real estate market, and the international Depression finally caught up with Edmonton and ended the boom period. And then World War I broke out. There was a feeling in this conservative city of ours that it was wrong to enjoy yourself when there was a war going on in Europe. Audiences fell off, and the mix of live theatre, vaudeville, and movies just wasn't attracting the size of audiences needed to keep the venture alive and healthy.

Things grew progressively worse for John McKernan. In 1919 the influenza epidemic reached Edmonton, and he was among the victims. He was weakened by his bout with the flu bug, contracted pneumonia, and died at his home at 11551 University Avenue on February 8, 1919. He was just short of his fortieth birthday.

The opening performance at the Princess back in 1915 featured Mary Pickford in a film called *The Eagle's Mate*.

There was another interesting advertisement that ran in the local papers on August 16, 1929. Three rival motion picture houses, the Rialto, the Empress, and the Capitol took out an ad congratulating the Princess on the introduction of "talkies." And the title of that first "talkie?" *The Canary Murder Case.*

On July 14, 1976, a plaque was put up that states:

In recognition of the elegance of its architecture, and of the place of the cinematograph in the cultural life of Alberta, the Princess Cinema was designated an historic site by the Hon. Horst A. Schmid, minister of culture.

This designation will help our stately Princess to remain for many more years to come.

Books in
the Big City

There are so many things in this city of ours that we take for granted, and one of them is the easy access we enjoy to books and libraries and reading. We have a happy history of books and libraries in Edmonton, and some very innovative "firsts" about which we can be proud. There was a biographical program on Andrew Carnegie on one of the cable television channels some time ago, but likely not all of the viewers realized that this famous old rascal had an impact on this city.

A group of Edmonton readers got together during the last few months of the nineteenth century and decided that they had best form a committee to look into the question of establishing some sort of library in town. That committee came into being on January 1, 1900, and we've never looked back.

The first library was more a place to sit and read rather than a separate building. A year after the committee was formed, on January 17, 1901, this first reading room opened in a building at 101 Street and Jasper Avenue.

A little more than a year later, in March of 1902, the Edmonton Public Library and Mechanics Institute came into being. With an impressive title like that, it was only a matter of time before it moved into the next stage of putting reading material into the hands of the town's citizens. In August of that same year, the new "library" opened two days a week in rooms rented in the McLeod Building in downtown Edmonton. The library must have been among the first tenants in Kenny McLeod's new building, because it wasn't fully completed until 1914. There were a grand total of eighty-five who signed up as members of this new institute, and for that privilege they each paid a membership fee of $3. That membership entitled each person to have access to the complete collection of the institute—one hundred books, sixteen newspapers, and a few magazines.

Our next formal library was located in the Chisholm Block, again in the heart of downtown Edmonton, at 104 Street and Jasper Avenue. It was on March 27, 1913, that the first books were circulated from that library in the Chisholm Block.

Across the river in Strathcona, things were moving ahead just as fast, if not faster. The Strathcona Public Library opened in March of the same year, and came into being thanks to a grant of $15,000 from Andrew Carnegie. This wealthy philanthropist was the financial spark behind the library building that's still in use on 104 Street at 84 Avenue.

In 1922, after some considerable negotiating, the Andrew Carnegie Corporation and the City of Edmonton announced that together they were going to finance and build a permanent library. The site had already been acquired in 1910 and reserved for a library building. It was right about where McCauley Plaza is today.

This new, permanent public library building officially opened August 30, 1923, and an interesting historical construction note enters the story. The new library building was constructed by a firm called Poole Construction, the first project of the new contracting firm headed by Ernest Poole.

On another historical note, it was the same firm, Poole Construction, that demolished the building forty-six years later. And it was Poole Construction again that built the AGT Tower on the same site. On the last day of September 1967, we moved into the new Centennial Library on Sir Winston Churchill Square.

The story of our library system in Edmonton isn't just a story of its buildings. For example, in 1941 the librarian, Hugh Gourlay, talked to the street railway people, and out of that conversation came North America's first streetcar library. It seems that other centres had used buses to move library books around, but Mr. Gourlay took the concept one step further, and the result was a converted streetcar that carried a comprehensive library to communities in a variety of areas in Edmonton.

It was on a Friday, October 10, 1941, that the first library car went on display at the corner of 101 Street and Jasper Avenue. Edmonton's Mayor Fry held an official opening that night, and a mere four days later, by October 14, more than five thousand people had already visited this moveable library.

The shelves down the inside walls of the car held fifteen hundred books, and the public library had purchased an additional three thousand new books to be used in the streetcar to keep the shelves stocked. The idea was to take the books to parts of the city where access to the downtown library was limited, and it worked more effectively than anyone had dared hope.

The first trip, out to Calder, took place on October 17, 1941, and the car was parked on a siding built for the purpose on 127 Avenue opposite the Canadian National Railway yards.

And how well did the new concept work? On the first day the library car was open from 3:00 PM until 9:00 PM and seven hundred people came to visit. Half of the callers were new customers, and what is even more significant is that 75% of the clients were children.

The same success story was told wherever the new service was offered. Another first for Edmonton, and a story that isn't often told.

Edmonton's
Stately Sentinel

Every year on July 5, there should be a major birthday party in downtown Edmonton, because one of this city's grand old ladies celebrates her birthday on that date, and she deserves to be honoured.

The Macdonald Hotel officially opened on July 5, 1915, and from what the newspapers of the time tell us, it was a night to remember. The hotel had been four years in the making, but it did the city proud when it was done. The hotel was part of the chain built by the Grand Trunk Pacific Railroad, and was designed in the style of a chateau. We even know some of the rather boring statistics that go with the structure. It cost about $2,225,000 to build and furnish, and those figures are in 1915 dollars. We also know that the hotel was faced with Indiana limestone and that the roof was covered with copper. But it is the story of that opening of the hotel that is so fascinating. Listen as the reporter begins his story about the opening in the *Edmonton Bulletin* issued the next morning, July 6, 1915:

> The Macdonald Hotel, the new Grand Trunk Pacific Hotel which was formally opened last night with a table d'hote dinner to which nearly five hundred guests sat down, is in its decorations, fittings, furnishings, and appliances, absolutely the last word in modern taste and invention, and the Edmontonians who had the privilege of inspecting it last night for the first time had nothing but praise for a building that for comfort, convenience, safety and appearance has few competitors on the continent.

The late Andy Snaddon, editor of the *Edmonton Journal*, had a hard and fast rule about the opening paragraph of any story: it must contain the nuts and bolts of the story, and it could not be longer than twenty-five words. Editorial standards must have been a little looser in 1915, because on the basis of word count alone, that paragraph comes in at eighty-one words.

Things moved more slowly in 1915, and the reader had more time to absorb detail, which was a good job because there is a tremendous amount of detail throughout the story. We learn, for example, that the hotel

> is at a point on the bank of the valley which sharply overlooks the water and commands a long view of river and valley, both up and down stream. From the south front the gentle, wooded slopes of the Beaver Hills rise in the near distance across the river, while the upper windows command a view of the city in every direction.

At this point in the story, the tour of the building begins, and the reporter didn't leave out a thing.

> The main doors are in the centre of the entrance portico, and are double, of the revolving type. The rotunda, paved with pink Lepanto marble, is spacious, as may be judged by its size of 56 x 45, and has a 25-foot oak beam ceiling. Here one may see a grandfather clock of the old-fashioned style, which is really an electric master clock connected with the clock system of the whole building. The master clock is synchronized with Greenwich time, and visitors may therefore compare their watches at any time and secure absolute accuracy of time.

That's a convenience you don't find in a lot of hotels these days, but you could get it at the Macdonald in 1915.

The reporter goes on to describe the lounge rooms across the rotunda from the main entrance, and mentions the roomy fireplace, above which hangs a large painting of the Fathers of Confederation, and in particular the first prime minister, Sir John A. Macdonald. And it is fitting that he mentions the late prime minister, since the hotel was named in his honour.

The architects, Ross and Macdonald of Montreal, get honourable mention in the story, as does the Canadian artist Arthur Hasley, also of Montreal. It was Mr. Hasley who designed and executed the decorative plastering. There is no mention in the story, though, of the young Scots decorative plasterer, John Leslie, who was trained in Edinburgh and also worked on the hotel. John Leslie was my grandfather, and I'm sure he was responsible for the finest of the decorative plasterwork throughout the building.

> The manager of the hotel is Louis Low, who has been on the ground for some time to see that the arrangements accord with the practical needs of hotel accommodation, and who will continue to direct its destinies.

And Edmonton needed a bright light somewhere in the news at that time. The country was in the middle of a world war, and things weren't going all that well. Just two months earlier German U-boats had torpedoed the *Lusitania*; she went down with more than one thousand people, 128 of them American. And just ten days before the big opening, the North Saskatchewan River had flooded, bringing disaster to the low areas of the river flats.

The newspaper that carried the detailed story of the Mac opening also carried a casualty list on the same page, a reminder of the war in Europe. Still another reminder of the new realities were the advertisements urging Canadians to send their quarters to the fund that had been set up to send tobacco and cigarettes to the troops overseas. You could help lessen the hardships of the battle line, you learned, if you just sent smokes to the boys.

But on a lighter note, another contemporary story advised that the Edmonton Newsboys Band had just about reached their goal of raising enough money to buy uniforms for the bandsmen. The amount subscribed reached $714.60, and one more push would do it.

That's the way we were, in 1915.

The Macdonald Hotel, seen here under construction in 1912, was named after Canadian Prime Minister Sir John A. Macdonald. Still one of the classier hotels in the land, it has housed the rich, the royals, and the famous over the years.

Flower Power
and the Paper

In 1919 the *Edmonton Journal* was using flower power and a strange slogan to promote the newspaper. Instead of saying, "Read the finest print," as it says today on all the benches at the bus stops, the *Journal's* motto was: "Every inch a newspaper." To emphasize its point, the newspaper decorated a 1919 touring car with flowers and drove it around town.

Starting another newspaper in Edmonton took a fair amount of self-confidence. Frank Oliver had started his *Edmonton Bulletin* in 1880, and it was a fairly well established newspaper in the area. But three newspapermen from Portage la Prairie, Manitoba, arrived in town in the fall of 1903, and they decided that Frank Oliver was about due for some good, old-fashioned competition.

When it's 1919 and you're advertising your newspaper, you might do what the Edmonton Journal *did and decorate an automobile with "flower power," illustrating the might of the press.*

Led by a fellow called John Macpherson, Arthur Moore and J. W. Cunningham helped to introduce the 5,500 people living in Edmonton at the time to what they called the *Evening Journal*.

Macpherson had run a daily paper in Portage la Prairie. He had fifteen years of experience behind him by that time. Arthur Moore was a reporter, and Cunningham was a print shop foreman. The three leased a small building behind the Empire Block, on 101 Street and Jasper Avenue. They started off as a print shop operation, but had the idea for a newspaper in mind right from the start. Their first edition appeared on November 11, 1903, and sold for a nickel. They printed one thousand copies.

There were some interesting stories that appeared in those early editions. In the November 26, 1903, issue of the paper, they reported: "Edmonton has added one more metropolitan feature to her appearance." The story went on to explain that the first electric sign in Edmonton had been turned on. They also reported that the official police census pegged the population of Edmonton at 5,445 souls.

There was a semi-weekly newspaper in Edmonton at the time, a paper called *The Edmonton Post*. That paper together with the *Bulletin* made up the *Journal*'s opposition, and on November 20, 1903, the *Journal* announced that it had bought the subscription list of *The Edmonton Post*, and *The Edmonton Post* stopped publishing.

In 1905 the paper moved to new quarters. The new offices were on a corner of the property that Robert Tegler owned, and upon which he was going to build his Tegler Building. The *Journal* was prospering and in 1908 showed a profit when their business year was completed, so they decided that they needed a building of their own. They bought a piece of land on 101 Street at the corner of 100 Avenue and proceeded to build their own quarters.

At the same time, Robert Tegler was forging ahead with his building, and wanted the property leased by the *Journal*. The newspaper wasn't ready to make the move to their new quarters; their lease was solid, and they decided to hang in there. Tegler, in his own strong-willed way, had his buildings designed so that he could go ahead with the construction, and built the structure over and around the newspaper offices. Then, when the lease had expired and the *Journal* had moved out, he demolished the old newspaper offices and completed the building the way he wanted it.

Macpherson, Cunningham, and another shareholder sold controlling interest in the newspaper in 1909, and three years later the Southam people bought the paper.

Never one to back down, the *Journal* found itself in a shoot-out with Alberta's Social Credit government in the fall of 1937. The Legislature had passed the Press Act on October 5, 1937, which, in effect, placed newspapers under government control. A front-page editorial appeared in the paper's edition of October 4, 1937, and the fight was on. The bill never did get assent and was overturned by the Supreme Court on March 4, 1938.

The front page of the May 2, 1938, issue of the *Journal* was a proud one for the paper. It was a wire story from New York that announced that the paper had received "a special public service Pulitzer prize in the form of a bronze plaque for its leadership in the defence of the freedom of the press in the Province of Alberta."

There were tough times on other fronts, as well. On May 30, 1946, the press room staff failed to report for work. There were labour troubles at the paper in Winnipeg, and the Edmonton printers went out in sympathy. In an unprecedented move, and with the press room staff off the job, the *Journal* and the *Bulletin* produced a joint issue of the two papers, and continued with this newspaper until normal labour conditions were restored.

We tend to take our local newspapers for granted in many cases, and it comes as a bit of a surprise to find that they have their own history. From that day back in 1880 when Frank Oliver brought Edmonton its first newspaper, right through until today, we have been served with a press that has been part of our community.

That tradition carries on, and part of the changing newspaper scene has been the appearance of weekly papers, bringing still another element to the reporting of the Edmonton story. Some of those papers include *The Real Estate Weekly*, *See*, and *Vue*. All of these papers tell, along with national and international articles, the stories behind the stories that make Edmonton the fascinating community it is today.

The University of Alberta's Proud Tradition

There is a photograph in the files of the City of Edmonton Archives that, at first glance, looks vaguely familiar. It shows what are referred to as the engineering buildings at the University of Alberta. It was taken in 1914, and all of the buildings shown are still in existence; it's just that they are surrounded by other buildings that are bigger, taller, and of a different style. The old familiar buildings aren't lost in the new scheme of things, but they are certainly overshadowed. It's when you start looking at the history of the university that you begin to realize how significant that photograph has become.

There was a turbulent period in our history when Edmonton learned that the transcontinental railway was not going to go through Edmonton on its way to the Yellowhead Pass and on to the Pacific. Instead, the railroad was going to be built through the Kicking Horse Pass, and Calgary was the Alberta centre that would be blessed with the rail connection to the rest of the world.

Edmonton's fight for a place in the geographic and political sun is an interesting one, and the part that Strathcona played in the drama is fascinating. Calgary got the railroad, true, but Edmonton got the provincial capital, and the university.

In 1899 the community south of the river became formally incorporated as a town. They needed a name, and they wisely decided to choose a director of the CPR as the man they wanted to honour. His name was Donald Smith, but they didn't want to call the new community Smith, so they moved to a title a little more grand. Donald Smith was also Lord Strathcona, and that's where the founding fathers of Strathcona got their name.

Time passed, things happened, and Strathcona grew. Strathcona became a city in March of 1907, with a population of 3,500. Then they set about doing all those things that a city does. They built a city hall and a fire hall, they built a library and a hospital, and they bought river lot 5, because they were going to have the University of Alberta on their side of the river.

Through all this, a gentleman called Alexander Cameron Rutherford became one of the key figures in the creation and development of the university. Rutherford was a lawyer and had come to the Strathcona area with his family in 1895. He took an active part in community affairs and local politics, and when Alberta became a province, A. C. Rutherford became the first premier. He urged the creation of the university, and on September 29, 1909, he turned the first sod in typical Rutherford style. None of this fiddling around with a mere shovel for A. C. Rutherford. He hooked the reins from four horses around his neck, and, grabbing the handles of a plough and clucking his tongue, he started the horses and *ploughed* the first sod instead of just turning it.

The history of the buildings on the campus is a little confusing. The first building completed there wasn't a university building at all; it was a Methodist theological college that operated as an arm of Alberta College. Today we know it as St. Stephen's College, and it, too, is still functioning on the campus.

During the early formative years, university classes were held on the second floor of Strathcona Collegiate Institute. That's another building that we're still using, but today we refer to it as the Old Strathcona High

A student rushing from one class to the next might not think about it, but the campus at the University of Alberta has changed a little since 1914.

School. When we put up buildings for educational purposes, we don't give up on them without a struggle.

The first university building completed that was actually on the campus proper was Athabasca Hall. It was formally opened in 1911 and housed the entire University of Alberta for the first few years.

Then the Arts Building and Convocation Hall came along, as well as the two separate laboratory buildings that flanked Con Hall on the west side of the Arts Building. These two laboratory buildings were given the sensible names of North Lab and South Lab. All four branches of engineering offered in the early years were housed in those two buildings. And there, across the quad, runs a wooden sidewalk that connected the residences with the labs and Con Hall.

And how big was the university in terms of students in those early years? Perhaps a good way to illustrate that would be to refer to the tea party that was held each year at the Rutherford home. The Rutherfords paid their regards to the entire graduating class by hosting a tea party at the Rutherford home on campus. This event became known as the Founder's Tea, and it was held until 1938, when there were five hundred guests in attendance.

A. C. Rutherford maintained his connection with the university over the years. He served as chancellor of the university from 1927 until his death in 1941. A proud tradition, indeed.

The Fantastic Photograph

It's not very often that we begin our look at an Edmonton story with a rather fuzzy photograph, but this time it's the photograph that is really the exciting part of the story.

The original picture was taken well over one hundred years ago. It turned up when a box buried under the cornerstone of an old church building was opened in 1925, and the more we look at the picture the more significant it becomes.

The building being razed when the cornerstone box was discovered was at one time the First Presbyterian Church in downtown Edmonton. This isn't the First Presbyterian Church we know today, the one on 105 Street south of Jasper Avenue, and it wasn't the *first* First Presbyterian Church in Edmonton, either. Perhaps we had best start right at the beginning and try and make sense out of this story.

It was on November 3, 1881, when twenty-two Presbyterians met in Jimmy McDonald's carpenter shop and talked about building a church. It was agreed that the construction of a church was in order, a constitution was adopted, a board of managers elected by democratic ballot, and regular services were organized and conducted by Reverend A. B. Baird. Those services were held on the second floor of the Capital Glass Works, located on the south side of Jasper Avenue at about 98 Street. Our convention centre sits there today, but over a century ago that was the second-storey location of First Presbyterian Church. First Presbyterian's first communion service was held upstairs at the Glass Works on May 18, 1882, with nine communicants taking part.

A year later, in November of 1882, the congregation had moved into their own building, a small wooden structure that held two hundred people. It was built on land donated by the Hudson's Bay Company at 104 Street and 99 Avenue. That wooden church was home to the Presbyterians for twenty years before they moved into a new, red-brick building on the southwest corner of 103 Street and Jasper Avenue. It was dedicated as the new First Presbyterian Church at a special service held on July 13, 1902. That building served the congregation for another ten years, at which point they moved into the present building on 105 Street.

When they laid the cornerstone for that building on 103 Street they looked around for significant things to place in the box to be buried under the cornerstone. The photograph in this story is the picture they chose to leave for future generations to examine and enjoy, but it deteriorated just a little over the years.

The picture was taken by C. W. Mathers, our first photographer. To take the photograph, he set up his tripod in the middle of Jasper Avenue and took the picture looking to the east. Mathers included in the picture such old established Edmonton businesses as Raymer's Jewellery store (it's the one with a clock for the outdoor sign over the front door), the Hudson's Bay Company, Mathers's studio, and the *Edmonton Bulletin* building. Also listed on the picture's record is something called the First Presbyterian Church.

But why would they include this particular photograph in their cornerstone box when they built the brick church on the southwest corner of 103 Street and Jasper?

Finding the answer was a little easier with the aid of a magnifying glass. The picture, over time, made its way from Mathers's studio into the Ernest

Old family albums turn up some strange pictures, but nothing quite like this 1887 photograph found under the cornerstone of an unidentified old building that was demolished in downtown Edmonton.

Brown collection. But somewhere along the line, somebody had taken a pen, dipped the nib into a bottle of ink, and written something across the bottom of the photograph. And that's where the answer to the riddle turns up.

The handwritten note tells us that the building on the extreme left behind the poplar trees is the workshop for James McDonald's carpenter shop. This picture shows the building where the original twenty-two Presbyterians met and discussed building a proper church. The picture also shows the general area where the Capital Glass Works business was located.

There are a number of photographs on file at the City of Edmonton Archives that show the laying of the cornerstone for the church on 105 Street, the one we know today as the First Presbyterian Church, and we're not sure whether there are any interesting photos buried under that cornerstone. We do know that one of the items under that stone on the 105 Street church is a bag of gold nuggets. As a classic example of Scots thrift, we can note here that those nuggets were found in the gravel that had been taken from the North Saskatchewan to mix the concrete that became the footings and foundation of this new church. And an interesting element of that cornerstone ceremony at the 105 Street church cries out for an explanation too. The cornerstone is on the second storey level, twenty feet in the air.

Well, this all makes sense if we remember that the first gatherings of the Presbyterians took place on the second storey of the Capital Glass Works building, so they were really just following tradition.

James Ramsey's Store

It was 1928 when an Edmonton businessman sold his store to an eastern firm for $1,000,000, and that's how Eaton's came to town. The businessman was James Ramsey, who had come to Edmonton in 1911 to make his fortune. Seventeen years later he cashed in on a dream and a lot of hard work.

But who was James Ramsey? Where did he come from? And what was the secret of his success? All of this becomes another chapter in the Edmonton story, but it's a chapter that has been without a great deal of recognition over the years.

James Ramsey came to Edmonton in 1911 and went into the retail business. We note in passing that he started out with $19,000 in capital. Fixtures accounted for $8,000 of that amount, freight $6,000, and expenses $5,000. The first day at Ramsey's they did $7,500 worth of business, and after that Ramsey survived an international depression and a world war before selling out for a fortune in 1928. One million dollars was a lot of money in 1928. It's a lot of money today, too.

Ramsey was born in Imlay City, Michigan, and his family moved to Canada when he was four years of age. They settled in Oxford County. James went to work at the age of thirteen in Plattsville, Ontario, and he kept sharpening his entrepreneurial skills for the rest of his life.

In the fall of 1910 he made a trip through western Canada looking for a good place to start a business. He looked at Moose Jaw, Regina, Saskatoon, Calgary, and Edmonton. He was quoted in a newspaper account as saying that he felt that Edmonton had by far the best business possibilities.

While he was in Edmonton he met another very keen business operator called Robert Tegler. Tegler had an idea for an office building in downtown Edmonton and talked to Ramsey about it. The building was still in the planning and design stage, but it sounded interesting to Ramsey. Before he left Edmonton, Ramsey asked Tegler to wire him the rental details and headed back east. Tegler sorted out his numbers and sent a proposal by telegram to Ramsey, who caught the next train back to Edmonton and signed the deal with Tegler. The rest, in a sense, is history.

Ramsey leased the ground floor of the Tegler Block on 101 Street and 102 Avenue. On opening day, James Ramsey Limited occupied 18,000 square feet of floor space, and there were sixty employees on the payroll. By 1926 the staff had grown to 312, and when Eaton's took over there were 337, rising to a seasonal high of 400 on the payroll.

And what made Ramsey's so successful? Many things, probably, but the most important one was Ramsey himself. He was an innovator. He looked for new ideas, new lines of merchandise, and new ways of marketing.

He travelled a great deal. Long before jet planes entered the business picture, Ramsey had circled the globe looking for items for his store. He visited every continent in the world except South America. Africa, Egypt, China, or Japan? He knew them all, and one estimate had him doing 800,000 miles of business travel.

Ramsey felt that not all of his potential customers could come to him, so he organized a mail order business that took his merchandise to the customers. Ramsey's had two regular mail order catalogues each year and two mid-season catalogues that went to out-of-town buyers. No matter where you lived, you could shop at Ramsey's at city prices.

James Ramsay came to Edmonton in 1911 and raised the art of merchandising to new heights in his department store in the heart of the city.

He may not have put it into so many words, but he believed in one-stop shopping. It was his philosophy that if there was anything you needed for your home, you should be able to buy it at Ramsey's.

Ramsey went to the spring stock show in Edmonton and bought all the prize-winning beef, then offered it for sale in the meat department, but he didn't increase the prices, and his customers knew that.

He paid his community dues as well. He served as an alderman on city council, as an MLA for his riding in East Edmonton, and he worked on and off for the Chamber of Commerce and the Board of Trade. He was a supporter of worthwhile causes in the city, and he brought his organizational skills into play when the Edmonton Stock Yards came into being.

All of this, we know, is interesting in itself, but we don't know very much about James Ramsey the person. When the Eaton's deal went through, he was quoted as saying that he had no firm plans for the future, except that he hoped to continue to live in Edmonton.

Is it any wonder that he was sometimes referred to as "Edmonton's Merchant Prince" but still remains a bit of a mystery man?

Bush Planes' Base

The Cree had a word for it, but it was a tricky one to work into a conversation. According to Eric Holmgren's book *2000 Place Names of Alberta*, the name given to the body of water by the Cree was *Opi-mi-now-wa-sioo*, but most Albertans find it easier to refer to it as Cooking Lake.

Cooking Lake sits about twenty miles to the east of us, and Eric Mardon, in his book *Community Names of Alberta*, tells us that, "In the days of the Red River Carts, it was on one of the major trails across the western prairies. Wagon trains used to stop here to cook a last meal before pushing on to Edmonton."

However the name originated, Cooking Lake has been a part of the life of Edmontonians since the early years of the city. There is one part of the Cooking Lake story that is often overlooked, though. The lake played an important role in the development of the use of airplanes in northern Canada. It was the summer terminus for the float-equipped bush planes that made their way in and out of the north.

Cooking Lake was a very popular summer resort for vacationing Edmontonians. A short drive from the city, even in a 1929 Chevrolet sedan, there was a happy combination of privately owned cottages as well as rental units that could be rented by the week. One of Edmonton's early hardware store operators, the man who owned Werner's Hardware, had built a cluster of cottages back from the beach front, and they served as the summer homes for many local families. A Werner's cottage was fairly basic. There was no glass in the windows, but there were canvas screens that could be rolled down for privacy or a sudden summer rain. Food was stored in a wooden box fitted into a pit just outside the cottage, and that was about the end of the amenities.

But for a small boy spending a couple of weeks at the lake, it was the complete summer holiday. It took only two minutes to dash through the bushes to the water's edge when a green and gold Mackenzie Air Service plane flew low overhead, before turning to land and taxi to the dock.

A little farther along the shore of South Cooking Lake stood the Lakeview Pavilion. This dates back to the days when people danced to the big band sounds of orchestras such as Mart Kenny's. The sound of the saxophones through the summer air at Lakeview was never to be forgotten, and in most instances, never replaced by any other instrument.

Then came the beginning of the development of the north, that part of it fuelled by the mobility of the planes that flew in and out with the ore and the furs, carrying in the equipment for the mines and the refineries. Landing and taking off in winter was no problem. Lakes were frozen, covered with snow, and so was the landing field at Edmonton. But during the summer there were no landing fields in the north, just the lakes, so the planes operated with floats rather than wheels or skis. And when they got back to the Edmonton area with their floats during those summer months, they landed at Cooking Lake.

The airport at Edmonton, the one we now call the Municipal Airport, was the first licensed airfield in Canada and given the odd name of the Edmonton Air Harbour. It was an arm of the Engineering Department and, as such, relied on the staff and equipment of the engineering people to open it up and keep it operating. A. W. Haddow, the city engineer, found $400 in one of his budgets and spent it clearing brush from the Edmonton airfield so it was easier, and safer, for the pilots to land.

The Cooking Lake airfield was also operated by the Engineering

The stories of bush pilots make a colourful chapter in Canadian history. Cooking Lake, shown here circa 1934, served as a summer home and airport to many of these fliers.

Department, and they based their operation across the lake from the beach area and the cottagers. They constructed a dock, they built a small lodge to accommodate the pilots and crews, and they put up the equipment that enabled the airplane's crews to hoist them off the ground and change from wheels to floats, or floats to skis, as the season's flying conditions dictated.

Nobody will ever know the fortunes in cargo that were unloaded at Cooking Lake. Nobody will ever know all of the stories that were told around the stone fireplace in the lounge at the lodge.

By today's standards, the facilities were basic. If a plane wanted to change to floats, it would fly from the Edmonton field and land on the short gravel strip at the lake's edge. It would taxi over to the hoist that would lift it into the air, the floats would be fitted, and the plane trundled down the dock and into the water on a rubber tired dolly. The same routine took place in the fall when it came time to put the skis back on for the winter trips.

There were surprisingly few accidents at the Cooking Lake base over the years. There was one incident in World War II when an RCAF flying boat hit a rock while approaching the dock at the base. The rock punched a hole in the plane's hull, but the pilot was able to beach the plane before it settled too far into the water and, apart from the hole that had to be patched, no great harm was done.

There's an airfield at Cooking Lake today, complete with a 2,950-foot runway, but it will never quite take the place of the original, when Edmonton first became "The Gateway to the North."

True
Champions

On June 15, 1915, a basketball team called the Commercial Graduates Basketball Club was formed, and when they closed down the club in 1940 they had played 522 games and won 502 of them. That means that they won 96% of the games they played. They dominated women's basketball all over the world while they were playing, and dominated is the operative word. What do the numbers 65–18, 88–11, 81–9, or 109–20 mean? Those are the final scores in some of the games the Grads played during their various tours. One year the Grads played against a team from Peterborough, Ontario. One-fifth of the population of Peterborough came out to see the game and they watched as the Grads took over. The final score in that Peterborough game? 107–6.

We call ourselves "The City of Champions," and in our minds we associate the title with hockey players, football teams, and other athletic accomplishments in relatively recent times. We tend to take the Grads for granted, and yet they set a world pace that has never been approximated, let alone beaten. And it all began in an Edmonton high school in 1914 under the guidance of one man: J. Percy Page.

Percy Page was a high school teacher who was interested in a wide variety of sports. In Edmonton he was teaching at the Commercial High School, where the student body was primarily young ladies training for a career in the business world. It was easier to put together a girls' basketball team than a boys' team, because there were a lot more girls.

There is a touch of confusion in the minds of Edmontonians as to just what year the team was formally started. To many sports fans, the Grads came into being in 1922. That's the year the team went east and came back as winners of the first Canadian Championship. But before that, you'll find that the Edmonton Commercial Grads were officially formed on that June date in 1915. And if you go just a little further back than that, you'll find that Percy Page had a girls' basketball team at the Commercial High School in 1914, and that it was at the end of their first year of playing that they made the move to formally become the Commercial Grads.

The name we take for granted actually has very simple roots. The team was based at the school at which Percy Page taught, the Edmonton Commercial High School. The players consisted of graduates of that school, so they called it the Edmonton Commercial Graduates Basketball Club, and of course it didn't take long to shorten that name to the Commercial Grads.

And who was Percy Page? He was born in Ontario and raised in the village of Bronte. He attended the Oakville High School before going on to Hamilton Collegiate Institute, which is where Percy Page first met the game called basketball. He continued his education at the Ontario Normal College and took a teaching position in St. John, New Brunswick. For five years he was on the teaching staff at the collegiate in St. Thomas and came to Edmonton in 1912 to assume the responsibility of commercial education on the north side of the river, and formed that first girls' team that played in 1914.

When it comes to the game of basketball it would seem that the world has forgotten just what a Canadian game it is. It was invented by a Canadian, Dr. James Naismith. And this may surprise you, but he was looking for a sport that could be played between the end of the football season and the start of the baseball season. And he found it all right. He nailed a peach basket to the wall of the gymnasium and had the students try to toss a ball into it. It seems almost too easy to say that the rest is history.

In 1936, the *Edmonton Journal* ran a picture story that talked of the two "greats" in the world of basketball. One was Naismith, the man who invented the game, and the other was J. Percy Page, the man who created a team and took it to world leadership.

Edmonton took the Grads to heart over the years. In 1928 the team went to Europe and the folks back home followed every move they made along their route. They sailed from Montreal on board the *Duchess of Argyll* on June 26. They visited London, Edinburgh, Paris, Marseilles, Nice, Monte Carlo, Rome, Florence, Milan, Berlin, and points in between. They arrived back here in Edmonton on August 31 of that year, and were given a royal welcome and celebrities' parade.

And while they were in London, they made a short side trip to meet another group of Edmontonians who happened to be in the neighbourhood. The Edmonton Newsboys Band was playing to a sell-out audience at Wembley Stadium and the Grads came to listen.

In an age when sports in general, and sports heroes as well, can be a little less than classic examples of the best, it is hard to imagine how J. Percy

Page could form a team and maintain its image and reputation from 1914 to 1940 without a blemish on the record.

It's all summed up in a quotation from a conversation with J. Percy Page in the *Calgary Herald* in 1932: "I have always insisted that a member of the 'Grads' must be a lady first, and an athlete second." That's why the Edmonton Commercial Grads were truly champions in the city of champions, and always will be.

The Story Behind
the Story

There are some fascinating chapters in the story of our city, and often we don't take the time to listen to the entire tale. When that happens, we often miss some of the more personal touches that are a very vital part of the event in question. Just such a story is told about the mercy flight made by Wop May and Vic Horner in early January of 1929. The two men flew vaccine to an isolated community in northern Alberta, and the story of that flight has been an integral part of Canadian aviation history.

There were all kinds of photographers on hand to record the return of the two fliers. We know that the weather was bitterly cold, that they were flying in an open cockpit airplane, and that they were completely exhausted when they arrived back in Edmonton. What we don't know is why Wop looks so terribly unhappy in all the photographs. He is normally a smiling, outgoing-looking person in all the pictures we see of him, and yet in all of the shots taken when the airplane landed back in Edmonton, he looks like the unhappiest pilot in the western world. And as you read this, you will probably be hearing the story behind Wop May's frown for the first time. It's the interesting part that fits on at the end of the rest of the story.

All of this began with a telegram that arrived sixty-six years ago. It was from Dr. H. A. Hamman in Fort Vermilion and was directed to the deputy minister of health for Alberta. The telegram read: "Logan, Hudson's Bay man at Red River, bad case of laryngeal diphtheria ... if possible rush airplane. Real emergency."

Dr. Malcolm Bow was the deputy minister of health at the time, and when he received the telegram he called Cy Becker at the Edmonton Flying Club. Becker said that there was an airplane that might make the trip, but it was an open cockpit Avro Avian. Commercial Airways of Alberta Limited owned the airplane. The two partners in Commercial Aviation were "Wop" May and Vic Horner. The Avian was sitting in a hangar at the Edmonton airport, and was fitted with wheels, not skis. And yes, the two partners were willing to make the flight to Fort Vermilion.

The Provincial Government came up with the anti-toxin requested by

Dr. Hamman, and on January 1, 1929, the two pilots took off and headed for Little Red River, about six hundred air miles north and west of Edmonton. There was a charcoal heater in the cockpit, not for the comfort of the pilots, but to keep the anti-toxin warm. This airplane had a seventy-five horsepower engine, so it wasn't the fastest machine in the world, but it was all that was available at the time.

On day number one the two fliers were hoping to make it to Peace River, but they didn't get away until 12:45 in the afternoon. The outside air temperature was at the minus thirty-five degree Fahrenheit level and the cloud level was so low that they spent the day flying only about five hundred feet above ground. On that first day they made it to McLennan, managing to land with what daylight there was left for them.

On day number two they took off from McLennan and stopped for fuel at Peace River. On take-off, they had to fly under the bridge over the Peace River, but they were on their way and made it to Fort Vermilion by 4:30 that afternoon. They delivered the anti-toxin to Dr. Hamman, but unfortunately, his patient had died.

The return trip to Edmonton wasn't any more pleasant than the trip north. The Avian made it back to Peace River, and the pilots landed with one gallon of fuel left in their tank.

The mercy flight made by Wop May and Vic Horner is legendary, but the story behind Wop May's frown is quite another matter.

165

They spent the night in Peace River, and the next day, Sunday, January 6, they flew back to Edmonton. They were so cold and stiff from their flight that after they had landed the two of them had to be lifted out of the cockpit of their airplane. They were given the heroes' welcome they so richly deserved. The newspaper reports of the epic flight tell us that ten thousand Edmontonians were at the airport to welcome the fliers on their return to the city. The papers tell us that Cy Becker of the Flying Club, too, took off to meet the Avian on its return to Edmonton, but had to turn back because of bad weather. Fox news even did a film feature on the two pilots after their safe return.

But up until now, nobody ever questioned the worried look on Wop May's face in all the photographs. Wop's son, Denny, tells us the reason.

Someone had told Wop May that if he wrapped a silk scarf across his face, the moisture from his breath wouldn't freeze. He tried it, and when he was landing at Edmonton, he pulled off the scarf and found that what he had been told wasn't true. The scarf had frozen to his lips, and when Wop May pulled it off, he ripped off the skin from his lips at the same time. That's why he looks so terribly unhappy, and now you know the story behind the story of the mercy flight to Fort Vermilion in 1929.

She Brought Us the Sound of Music

I t was on January 6, 1935, on a frosty Edmonton night, when eight people gathered to talk music. By the time the evening was over, the Edmonton Civic Opera Society had been formed.

The meeting was held at the home of Mrs. J. B. Carmichael. She and her husband, one of the city's more prominent dentists, lived at 10012 - 106 Street, in the heart of downtown Edmonton. And it was Mrs. Carmichael who brought the sound of music to the city, and made Edmonton sing.

She was born Beatrice van Loon in South Bend, Indiana, but throughout her life her close friends called her Auntie Van. Auntie Van died in that house on 106 Street on March 11, 1964, but she brought a great deal of delightful music to Edmonton audiences over the twenty-nine years that passed since that inaugural meeting of the Edmonton Civic Opera Society.

As is often the case with people who have such an impact on a city's development, the story of how Beatrice van Loon wound up in Edmonton is one of the lesser-known chapters of her colourful life. She seemed destined for a musical career all her life; she first performed on stage at the age of four and had sung in a number of American cities by the time she was eleven. She studied violin and piano until she turned seventeen, and then began a serious study of German and Italian while continuing her training as a singer. This young lady was headed for the opera stage. After studying opera in Chicago and New York for four years and mastering eight roles in German opera, she was about to sail for Europe to sing professionally in Germany when she was suddenly forced to change her plans. The year was 1914: the First World War had erupted, and Beatrice stayed in America. She played, she sang, she studied, and she began to conduct.

In 1919, Beatrice was sitting in front of a map of Canada trying to find a place called Edmonton. She was the conductor of a girl's orchestra, and they had just signed a contract to perform at a place called the Macdonald Hotel in Edmonton, Alberta. Her father said that she could go, but that she must not, under any circumstance, expose her face to the freezing temperatures she was bound to encounter.

*The talented Mrs. J. B. Carmichael, on her way to Europe to pursue
operatic studies, made a side-trip to Edmonton that never ended;
her legacy for Edmontonians is a score of musical memories.*

Beatrice van Loon led her orchestra to Edmonton, but ended up staying here. She had met an English dentist by the name of J .B. Carmichael, and they were married in 1920.

Mrs. Carmichael was so unique in this city that in 1929 the *Edmonton Bulletin* sent a reporter to interview her. At the time, she was the only woman playing with the Edmonton Symphony Orchestra, where she was first violinist. In addition to teaching voice and violin, she was also directing two other local orchestras: the University Orchestra and another group known as the Radio Orchestra, because it played regularly on the radio station CKUA. She also staged a regular concert each year for the Victorian Order of Nurses, and produced a yearly opera at the university. And she did all of these things on top of her regular duties and responsibilities as the symphony's lead violinist.

But her name is still best known in Edmonton musical circles for the regular productions of the Edmonton Civic Opera Society. The first one, "Maritana," was staged in 1935 in the old Empire Theatre. There were twelve principals, a chorus of thirty-eight, an orchestra of thirty, and Mrs. Carmichael, who served as the music director. The production lost money, but Mrs. Carmichael covered the deficit out of her own pocket and kept the Opera Society going. Over the next ten years, they reached out to Edmonton audiences. Some of the early offerings included "Faust" in 1937 and "Carmen" in 1940.

The society transferred their productions to the Strand Theatre in 1943 and presented their productions from that stage before moving on to the Jubilee Auditorium and another presentation of Carmen in 1957.

Gauging that Edmonton audiences were more inclined towards light opera, by the early 1960s the society was producing works ranging from "Most Happy Fella" to "The Music Man." The list of names of Edmontonians who performed in Civic Opera Society productions is incredible, and the lessons learned under the baton of Mrs. Carmichael did carry some of the performers on to professional careers, but for most the Opera Society served as an element of music in their lives in Edmonton.

The production of "The Music Man" in 1962 had a fellow called Dalt Elton playing Professor Harold Hill, the leader of the band. Dalt was the boss at the radio station CJCA at the time, before being moved later to a sister station in Vancouver. Playing opposite Elton was another Edmontonian who went on to make a name for himself in another field, Steve Paproski, who served as a Member of Parliament until his death. "The Music Man" was Mrs. Carmichael's last production, and was felt by many to be her finest.

Perhaps the most significant element in the entire story of the Edmonton Civic Opera Society wasn't really told until after Mrs. Carmichael's death in 1964. Part of the story run by the *Edmonton Journal* on the day of her funeral read:

> The company she founded was a remarkable institution. It has produced grand light operas for 29 years, given sound training to thousands of performers, given scholarship aid to singers and musicians of promise, raised more than $2,500 for war charities, and provided enjoyment and a cultural outlet to tens of thousands of Edmontonians. But remarkably, it remained an amateur company, drawing mainly on local talent and bringing in only an occasional outside star for major performances.

> The record may well be unsurpassed in North America and is a standing tribute to the remarkable capacity and unselfish devotion of Mrs. Carmichael.

Emergency Response History

When you're telling the story of the emergency response teams in Edmonton you could say that it starts in a poolroom and ends in a ballroom. That wouldn't be absolutely correct, although a poolroom and a ballroom do play a part in the story.

Part of the emergency response department is, of course, our ambulance service, and that did have its beginning in a pool hall. It was back in 1911, on a Wednesday night, and Norman Symonds was enjoying a quiet game of billiards at Deacon White's Pool Room. Deacon White's was a popular spot. He was a sportsman who was largely responsible for the introduction of rugby football in Edmonton. The first rugby games were played at Diamond Park, in the same place you'll find Telus Field today, and you might be interested to know that it was Deacon White who put together a rugby football team in 1921 that he called the Edmonton Eskimos. The Esks whipped Calgary and Winnipeg that year and went east to play the Toronto Argonauts, but we won't get into a conversation about the score in that game. The Esks lost.

Back at the poolroom that night, Mr. Symonds suffered an epileptic seizure. The ambulance arrived, but too late, and Mr. Symonds died in hospital. This brought to a head the cry for a patrol wagon for the police department: a wagon that could do double duty. It would not only transport the wayward to the police station when needed, but could be pressed into service as an emergency vehicle, or in other words, as a motorized ambulance. This was such a good idea that city council acted on it right away, but it took two years before the wagon arrived.

When it finally arrived at the end of January 1913, the vehicle was referred to as the Kissel Wagon. They called it that because it had been manufactured by the Kissel Kar Motor Company of Hartford, Wisconsin. It was built on a one-ton chassis, had a fifty horsepower motor and even an electric starter.

Prior to the acquisition of the Kissel Wagon we did have an ambulance service, and that too, is an interesting part of our history.

The earliest ambulance service we had was a horse-drawn unit. If you got sick and needed help getting to the hospital you phoned the fire department. The call was forwarded to the old fire hall on 104 Street, just south of Jasper Avenue. A team of horses was hitched up to the ambulance and help was on its way. You might be interested, too, to discover that the very first real ambulance we had here in Edmonton wasn't purchased by the City. It was bought by the Westward Ho! chapter of the Daughters of the Empire and donated to the City to operate.

There was a time between 1913 and 1933 when each undertaker in Edmonton ran an ambulance service along with their regular operation. This is, perhaps, a little startling to think about, but nevertheless it worked well.

These were the Depression years, and people turned their hand to whatever work they could find. Sherman Maxwell Smith went to work for Howard and McBride's Funeral Home in 1931 where one of his jobs was to drive the Howard and McBride ambulance. Then Jock McNeill came into the picture. There had been a McNeill's Taxi, Storage and Moving Company for years. Then, in 1933, Jock bought all the ambulances from the undertakers and made them part of his taxi fleet. One of the drivers retained by Jock was Mr. Smith. That was fine for a few years, and then in 1936 Sherman Maxwell Smith in his turn bought all the ambulances from Jock McNeill, and Smith's Ambulance Service was born.

In 1953 Smith was growing a little weary of the intensity of the business, so he signed the City Ambulance Contract with the City of Edmonton under Mayor William Hawrelak, and the city took over a lot of the paperwork. The cost of an ambulance trip jumped from $3 to $8.

In 1955, after a long and heated series of debates, the City decreed that Smith could continue to operate the ambulances, but the City would provide an intern from the Royal Alex Hospital to be in charge of each unit when it went out on an emergency call. The difficulty here was that while the interns were skilled in the world of medicine, they were not so skilled at driving an emergency vehicle through traffic when responding to a call.

More time passed, and with Mr. Smith battling failing health, he sold his ambulance service. He died on February 9, 1975.

In June 1981, the City took the various pieces of the ambulance service and put them all together, out of which came the Edmonton Ambulance Authority, which in turn became part of the emergency response department we have today.

There was a time when all you needed to work on an ambulance was a

first aid certificate, but that of course has changed, and we now have para-
medic training available at the institute of technology level. Added to this
training is a recent innovation, and one that is now being copied all across
Canada. It's called the Cadet Program, and was originated by John Simpson
of our emergency response department. This program takes Edmonton's
youth and puts them into a training program geared toward preparing them
for a career in the business of caring for Edmontonians. It operates under
the guidance of a committee that includes the parents of the cadets. The
cadet program had its first fund-raising dinner on June 13, 1997.

It's been a long trip from Deacon White's Pool Room to the Crowne
Plaza Ballroom, where the cadet program dinner was held, but Edmonton
has been a leader all along the way in the world of emergency response.

Edmonton's Kissel Wagon sits between the police car and two department
motorcycles, the ultimate in emergency response vehicles in 1913.

Mr. Reynolds
Comes to Town

At three minutes to two on the afternoon of Tuesday, April 15, 1947, Mr. Milton Reynolds dropped in on his way to New York City and things around here haven't been the same ever since.

Mr. Reynolds was the third man in a converted World War II, twin-engine bomber. The plane flew around the world in a record-breaking seventy-eight hours, fifty-five minutes, and fifty-eight seconds. Mr. Reynolds flew facing backwards during the entire flight, and he only stopped in Edmonton for sixty-nine minutes, but none of this has anything to do with the way Mr. Reynolds changed our thinking or our habits.

Mr. Reynolds was a pen manufacturer in New York. He bought the bomber and converted it to make it suitable for long range flights. To fly it he hired two men, pilot William Odem and flight engineer Carroll "Tex" Salee, and he spent $175,000 in hard-earned, 1947 dollars to make this record-breaking flight.

They took off from La Guardia field in New York, on a Saturday afternoon. They touched down at Gander, Newfoundland, flew over Shannon in Ireland, and landed in Paris. From Paris they flew to Cairo, from Cairo to Karachi, and from Karachi to Calcutta. From Calcutta they flew over to Shanghai and then on to Tokyo. Then it was up to Ada, Alaska, after which it was down the old Northwest Staging Route to the municipal field here in Edmonton, sometimes called Blatchford Field. They touched down on the runway in Edmonton at 1:57 PM on that afternoon in 1947.

And what was all this in aid of? Well, remember that Mr. Reynolds was a pen manufacturer. He was also somewhat of a salesman, and as he flew around the world he handed out samples of a new kind of pen that he was manufacturing. It would write through butter, he claimed, it wouldn't leak into your shirt pocket, you could shake it in somebody's face and the ink wouldn't spatter them. In fact, you didn't even have to fill it with ink.

It didn't have a conventional nib, the way pens were supposed to have. Reynolds's pen had a small metal ball in place of the nib. The ink was stored in the barrel of the pen, so when you put the pen to paper and moved it across the page, the metal ball became coated with ink and transferred the ink to the piece of paper. And of course Mr. Reynolds called his new invention the ballpoint pen.

And that's how it all began. Mr. Reynolds didn't give away all his pens; he sold most of them for $5 apiece. This was 1947, and you could get a Parker or a Waterman's fountain pen for that kind of money. But Mr. Reynolds's revolutionary new pen caught on, and where would we be today if it weren't for ballpoint pens?

The Reynolds's flight got a lot of media coverage. The front page of the *Edmonton Bulletin* on Wednesday, April 16, had big pictures of the refuelling process in front of the main terminal at the Municipal Airport, but neither Mr. Reynolds, nor his plane, nor his pen, made the headlines. An explosion in Texas City, Texas, that levelled the city and took 350 lives was the lead story.

Things were busy down at city hall that April. Council put the stamp of approval on a system called daylight saving time, and declared in its wisdom that it would start on April 27 and run right through until September 28. The big news out of London, England, had to do with the royal family. A reliable source in Buckingham Palace was quoted as saying that according to the highest authorities, the engagement of Princess Elizabeth, heir presumptive to the British throne, and Lieutenant Philip Mountbatten was about to be announced.

If you were downtown that day, you might have popped into Woodward's Groceteria and picked up some staples for the pantry. Netted gem seed potatoes were on sale for $2.15 a sack. Gladiola bulbs were on for six for fifty cents, and Texas Ruby Red grapefruit were at six for twenty-five cents.

Teapots were on sale for forty-five cents, and ladies' dress shoes were offered at $1.69. Oxfords for boys and youths were there for ninety-eight cents a pair.

If you were reading the paper that day, you might have spotted the item in the "Ripley's Believe It Or Not" column that a plough had been found imbedded in a tree on the Zeffinwell farm in Iowa, and that Delaware was the only state in the union that was free of rattlesnakes.

There were lots of comics for your entertainment: Dick Tracy, Moon Mullins, Superman, Gasoline Alley, Archie, Freckles and his friends, Steve Canyon, Orphan Annie, Alley Oop, or Major Hoople.

If you felt like taking in a movie, there was *The Chase*, playing at the Rialto, starring Robert Cummings, Michele Morgan, and Peter Lorre. The

Capital was showing *Notorious*, with Cary Grant and Ingrid Bergman. At the Avenue, Joan Crawford was the big star in *Mildred Pierce*.

Or if you wanted to work in the yard that weekend you could pick up a brand new, push-type lawn mower at the Bay for $15.95.

But it was a lot more fun just to sit at the kitchen table and see whether your brand new ballpoint pen would really write through a layer of butter.

Edmonton's Drive-in Theatres

It was Monday evening, June 6, 1949, and Edmonton's first drive-in theatre opened for business. It was the beginning of an era, and at the height of it all Edmonton laid legitimate claim to being the drive-in theatre capital of the country. By 1977 we had ten of these outdoor theatres in town, more than any other Canadian city. Person and Routledge tell us, in their book *Edmonton: Portrait of a City*, that Toronto had six, Winnipeg had five, and Saskatoon had four. So there you go—Edmonton leading the pack again.

It's probably not a fair thing to lay on the operators, but there was almost something prophetic about the film they chose to run that opening night: *The Time, The Place and the Girl*. The drive-in theatres had somewhat of a reputation, and there was a time when they were referred to by the unkind as "passion pits." Not that the name didn't have some merit. One of the operators talked about the night they lost the sound for over thirty minutes and nobody seemed to notice. At least nobody blew his or her horn in protest.

That first theatre, the Starlite, was on 156 Street at 87 Avenue, and back in 1949 it was out in the country. No Meadowlark Shopping Centre, no high-rise residences, not even a thought about a West Edmonton Mall.

It's hard to say just why drive-in theatres were so popular in Edmonton. The original appeal was to families. The first advertisements touted the fact that you didn't need to find a babysitter. Load the kids in the back of the car and away you go. If they fell asleep before the film was over that was fine, too. You could wake them up when you got home. You could smoke if you liked, and you certainly couldn't do that in a downtown theatre. You could wear your most comfortable old clothes, and if you were on an economy drive you could bring your own popcorn. You could even bring the family dog, if he didn't like to stay at home alone.

There was a snack bar, though, and bathroom facilities. You may not remember the details, but you paid your admission, drove in, and picked a stall in which to park. And then you leaned out the window of the car and unhooked the speaker that was hanging on a post. You clipped the speaker to the top of the window glass on the car and rolled up the window to hold it in place. There was a volume control, and when the film started you could set the sound level in your own private theatre. It was marvellous.

There are some valid questions that arise in the minds of people today who weren't there to enjoy the delights of drive-ins. What did you do in the wintertime when the temperature was forty below? How could you see the screen in July when it didn't get dark until after 10:00 PM?

There were in-car heaters, true, but the drive-ins were a warm weather form of entertainment, and the daylight didn't seem to be that much of a problem. The layout was always such that the screen was reasonably visible, even on a bright evening.

The screen at the Starlite measured forty-five feet by fifty-seven feet, and the supporting structure was seventy feet high. The Starlite could accommodate one thousand cars and was a success from its first day in 1949.

The Belmont Drive-in opened in 1954, and it featured what was believed to be the first curved screen in Alberta. Hot on the heels of that development, the Twin-Drive-in Theatre opened in Namao, and it was built to show wide-screen films. Their screen stood forty feet high and was one hundred feet wide—the largest screen in North America when it opened.

Edmonton was the drive-in theatre capital of Canada at one time.

And what else was going on in town in June 1949? Well, first of all you didn't have to go to a drive-in to see a movie. Randolph Scott was in *Canadian Pacific* at the Capital, and at the Rialto Dick Powell and Elizabeth Scott were starring in *Pitfall*. You could also go to the Varscona, the Roxy, the Avenue, or the Gem.

If you were interested in the latest in sound reproduction for the home, you could always go downtown and listen to the most recent RCA product on the market. They called it the amazing new playing system that "brings you better music at less cost." This was the introduction of forty-five rpm discs, and there aren't too many of them around today, either.

In the world of clean clothes, Woodward's was offering a Simplicity washing machine, wringer and all, for $144.50.

One of the news stories announced that it was likely that Alberta wouldn't have television for another five years, and on the crime front, water pistols in the hands of wayward youths were a problem in city playgrounds.

The papers also carried a story about a proposed addition to the Macdonald Hotel. It was to be sixteen storeys high, which would make it the tallest building in Edmonton.

And if you turned to the comic pages, you could enjoy Dick Tracy, Mary Worth, Orphan Annie, Alley Oop, and Gasoline Alley. There were some new strips on the page as well, with names such as Steve Canyon, but the old favourites, like Gasoline Alley, were still there with Major Hoople and Out Our Way down in the corner of the page.

But it was a big summer at the drive-in theatre, with bigger and better things to come over the next few years. It was 1949, and Edmonton's world was changing.

Drama in Real Life

When newspapers, radio, and television coverage bring us stories of violent crimes in other parts of the continent, we have a tendency to think that it could never happen here. It can, though, and it has happened, right here in Edmonton.

At 12:16 AM on the morning of February 22, 1950, in the Fort Saskatchewan jail, two trap doors opened at the same time and two men dropped to their death at the same moment. That was the last time capital punishment occurred in this part of the world. The two men who died that morning were Michael Joseph Hayes and Wilfred Leslie Nowell.

On the last day of June 1949, a drinking party in West Jasper Place turned violent. It all started out innocently enough as the gathering got going at the home of Michael Hayes. His wife was there, and so were two other men, Buster Robbins and William McKay. McKay had some cash and Hayes wanted it, so a fight broke out. It turned violent when Hayes hit McKay first with a length of lead pipe, and then an axe. McKay was robbed of his money, all of $118.00. He was dragged from the house and buried in a shallow ditch in Hayes's garden. He may very well have still been alive at the time. Hayes's wife had tried to intervene when the attack took place, but Robbins restrained her.

The party continued, and the following afternoon Mrs. Hayes convinced her husband that he should go and get his hair cut. As soon as he left the house, she phoned the police and told them what had happened. When Hayes came back from the barbershop in a cab, he told the driver that the hole being dug in the front yard, a hole seven feet long, three feet wide, and four feet deep, was for a water reservoir. Hayes was arrested at the scene, after which he was tried, found guilty, and sentenced to hang.

Three weeks after this grisly affair took place, an angry employee made his way into the office of his boss and shot him with a borrowed Luger pistol. The boss was Thomas Law, and the firm was Law Brothers Signs. The employee was Wilfred Leslie Nowell.

The shooting took place in the offices of Law Brothers Signs, which

179

happened to be right next door to the city police station. Response time was measured in seconds, and with Nowell still on the premises, the police made a quick arrest. Nowell stood trial, and he, too, was found guilty and sentenced to be hanged at the Fort Saskatchewan jail.

All of this sounds like the sort of thing you might read on the front page of a tabloid paper while you wait for your groceries to be checked through at the supermarket. But we forget, as a rule, that real people are involved, and there is a terribly sad sequel to the story of Wilfred Leslie Nowell. Nowell had been a commercial artist throughout his working career. He drew things and painted things. This was his life. And suddenly he found himself locked up in the death cell, all alone, in the Fort Saskatchewan jail.

Nowell was supplied with a few magazines—*Time, Life,* that sort of thing—the news magazines of the day. And Nowell had with him a small wooden pencil.

After the execution had taken place that February morning in 1950, a check of Nowell's cell showed that he had spent part of his time drawing on the wall. With his pencil, he had copied the portraits of the people who had been pictured in the news magazines he had been reading. They were draw-

There are sad chapters in the history of any city. One of Edmonton's sadder ones is the story behind a collection of drawings found on the wall of the death cell at the Fort Saskatchewan jail.

ings of the newsmakers of the day, some famous, some not. There was the Pope, Franklin Roosevelt with his cigarette tilted up against the world, and General Montgomery. There were eight people in all, three women and five men. They were there, in black pencil lines, on the grey concrete wall of the cell.

The cell was repainted very quickly, but not before one of the guards at the jail took a photograph of the sketches on the concrete wall. And that photograph is all that remained of the presence of the man who had been in that cell and made those drawings.

Time passes, life goes on, and we forget about the people behind the stories that make all those headlines. But they are real people, whatever their tragic endings, even if all we have to remember them is a photograph of some pencil drawings on the wall of a death cell.

The Mailman's
Arrival

You may be surprised to find that postal service in Edmonton goes back more than 125 years. It was on March 1, 1874, that Richard Hardisty began multi-tasking as the chief factor here at Fort Edmonton, and as the postmaster, as well. Since it took an ox cart three months to reach here from Winnipeg, the mail was a little slow in getting from one place to another, but that was when we first had postal service here in town.

Another major date in the history of mail service in Edmonton is June 1, 1907. On that date in history, seven intrepid mail carriers headed out on their appointed rounds and gave us twice-daily postal service right to our front doors. All it took to give us that twice-a-day delivery service were seven postmen. We were the only city between Winnipeg and Vancouver to have this luxury, although Calgary picked up on the idea and started it the next day, June 2.

There was a photograph taken of the Group of Seven, along with the postmaster of the day, Mr. Alexander E. May. Mr. May had two sons, Court and Wilfred. Wilfred is better known as "Wop" May, a name known in aviation circles all over the world.

The letter carriers had their problems, though. The houses didn't have numbers on them, many of the streets weren't identified, and people using the mail weren't used to putting complete addresses on the envelopes. The population wasn't used to the sight of a uniformed postal worker, either. One of the mailmen went into a Chinese laundry, according to a newspaper account of the day, only to have the proprietor throw up his hands and shout, "Don't take me! I'll pay." Just what he thought was happening we can only guess.

All in all, 1907 wasn't a happy year for the postal service. It got off to a good start with the introduction of door-to-door delivery, and it also moved into a nice new building on the northwest corner of 100 Street and 101A Avenue. But at about noon on October 17 somebody noticed smoke coming up through the floor registers of the new post office, and the fire that had started in the basement was almost out of control by the time the fire brigade arrived on the scene. The building was a total loss, but luckily very little mail was destroyed in the fire.

The building that went up in flames was actually the third post office building we'd had over the years. The first post office as a separate building went up in 1883. It was built on the piece of land now occupied by the *Edmonton Journal* building on 101 Street and Macdonald Drive. It was a two-storey structure, with the post office on the ground floor, and the postmaster, A. D. "Dad" Osborne, living upstairs. He got from his working area to his home by climbing a ladder to the second floor.

On July 1, 1883, the first shipment of mail left this new post office building and headed for the outside world. It was loaded on a stagecoach headed for Calgary. The route was down the hill to John Walter's ferry, across the river, and then south through the Peace Hills (Wetaskiwin) area, on past the Battle River, the Red Deer River, and finally to Calgary. It took five days to make the trip. If you were a passenger on the stagecoach your fare was $25, and you brought your own bedding. After all, you were on the road for four nights and five days, and you had to sleep somewhere. We'd had mail delivery on the steamer *Northcote* since 1875 but only during the months when the river was open. This stagecoach trip marked the first regular, overland service.

That first post office must have been well built. It was moved from the 101 Street location to a spot on the top of the riverbank about where the convention centre sits today. Then it was moved to the back of a lot at 9923 106 Street. Mr. Osborne's son, Colonel Osborne, owned the property and he used the buildings as a garage.

In 1936, it was decided to tear down the structure. It's a shame, but things like first post offices weren't fully appreciated at the time. The workmen found some old Toronto newspapers dating from 1881 to 1883 when they were wrecking the building.

It's sad to think what we lost with the destruction of that building. Inside the "garage" they found a wooden drop-letter box with a hand-carved opening at the top. It had been nailed to the outside of the post office so that Edmontonians could drop off their outgoing mail. There was a hand-made lock on the box as well.

In 1935, at one of the low points in the Depression, a proposal was brought forward to move the structure to the exhibition grounds, setting it up next to the Old Timers' Cabin. A story in the *Edmonton Journal* on July 2, 1936, concludes with a very sad entry: "Owing to the expense involved in such an operation, it was decided that the building could not be moved."

We had another post office on Jasper Avenue beside Graydon's Drug Store before we had the one that burned down, and then came the beautiful structure where the Westin Hotel stands today, and at least we've preserved the old clock from that building.